History for NI Key Stage 3

Ireland
1500–1900

- **Sheelagh Dean** • **Cheryl Stafford** • **Catherine Thompson**

HODDER
EDUCATION
PART OF HACHETTE LIVRE UK

The Publishers would like to thank the following for permission to reproduce copyright material:
Photo credits **p.8** *tl* © Geoff Caddick/epa/Corbis, *tc* Chris Djukanovic/Express/Getty Images, *tr* © Frank May/epa/Corbis, *bl* AP/PA Photos, *bc* Jeff J Mitchell/Getty Images, *br* bobo/Alamy; **p.13** *tl* © Walker Art Gallery, National Museums Liverpool/The Bridgeman Art Library, *tr* © British Library Board. All Rights Reserved/The Bridgeman Art Library, *bl* 'Mary Rose', Henry VIII's Ship by Willis, Richard (contemporary artist) Private Collection/The Bridgeman Art Library, *br* Authors Image/Alamy; **p.17** *tl* © Krause, Johansen/Archivo Iconografico, SA/Corbis, *bl* © Krause, Johansen/Archivo Iconografico, SA/Corbis, *tr* Stock Montage/Getty Images, *br* Visual Arts Library (London)/Alamy; **p.18** © Charles & Josette Lenars/Corbis © Banco De Mexico, Diego Rivera and Frida Kahlo Museums Trust, Av. Cinco de Mayo No. 2, Col. Centro, Del. Cuauhtemoc, 06059, Mexico, D.F. Courtesy del Instituto Nacional de Bellas Artes y Literatura, Mexico; **p.20** North Wind Picture Archives/Alamy; **p.22** Virginia Historical Society, Richmond, Virginia; **p.28** The Flight of the Earls – The Departure of Hugh O'Neill (c.1540–1616) from Ireland (oil on canvas) by Ryan, Thomas (b.1929) Private Collection/© Thomas Ryan RHA/The Bridgeman Art Library; **p.29** *l* Reproduction by kind permission of An Post ©, *r* © Belleek Pottery; **p.32** MS 634 ff.73-74 © Lambeth Palace Library, London, UK/The Bridgeman Art Library; **p.33** MS 634 ff.79v-80 © Lambeth Palace Library, London, UK/The Bridgeman Art Library; **p.34** © David Jones; **p.35** Private Collection/The Bridgeman Art Library; **p.36** © Museum of London, UK/The Bridgeman Art Library; **p.37** © Tony Crowley/Claremont Colleges Digital Library; **p.41** *t* © The Art Archive/Corbis, *b* The Print Collector/Alamy; **p.42** *t* © Bill Rolston author of *Drawing Support 3: Murals and Transition in the North of Ireland*, Belfast, Beyond the Pale Publications 2003, *b* Private Collection/The Bridgeman Art Library; **pp.44–5** Reproduced with the kind permission of the Northern Ireland Assembly, photograph by Chris Hill; **p.47** Published by BBC Books, reprinted by permission of The Random House Group Ltd; **p.48** *t* Emerald Music (Ireland) Limited, *b* Courtesy of Aida Yared, www.joyceimages.com; **p.51** *tl* © Bettmann/Corbis; *tr* The Art Archive/Musée Carnavalet Paris/Alfredo Dagli Orti, *b* Private Collection/The Bridgeman Art Library; **p.53** *t* Private Collection/Ken Welsh/The Bridgeman Art Library, *tc* © Bettmann/Corbis, *bc* Yale University Art Gallery, New Haven, CT, USA/The Bridgeman Art Library, *b* Hulton Archive/Getty Images; **p.54** *t* Yale University Art Gallery, New Haven, CT, USA/The Bridgeman Art Library, *b* © PoodlesRock/Corbis; **p.55** © Brooklyn Museum/Corbis; **p.56** Chateau de Versailles, France/Giraudon/The Bridgeman Art Library; **p.57** Bibliotheque Nationale, Paris, France/Giraudon/The Bridgeman Art Library; **p.61** *t* © Leeds Museums and Galleries (Lotherton Hall) U.K./The Bridgeman Art Library, *c* Private Collection/The Bridgeman Art Library, *b* Private Collection/Peter Newark Historical Pictures/The Bridgeman Art Library; **p.62** *t* Mary Evans Picture Library, *c & b* Courtesy of the National Library of Ireland; **p.66** *tl* © Shannon Stapleton/Reuters/Corbis, *tc* akg-images, *tr* © Mike Alquinto/epa/Corbis, *bl* Brian Lawrence/Rex Features, *bc* AP Photo/Curtis Compton/PA Photos, *br* © Mc Pherson Colin/Corbis Sygma; **p.68** Illustrated London News; **p.69** *t* © Hulton-Deutsch Collection/Corbis, *bl* © National Portrait Gallery, London, *br* © National Portrait Gallery, London; **p.70** *t* Hulton Archive/Getty Images, *b* © Office of Public Works, Dublin; **p.71** *t* Mary Evans/Mary Evans ILN Pictures, *b* Mary Anne McCracken (1770–1866) Photograph © Ulster Museum 2008 Collection Ulster Museum, Belfast. Reproduced courtesy of the Trustees of National Museums Northern Ireland; **p.72** © Illustrated London News/Mary Evans; **p.73** Joe Fox/Alamy; **p.76** © Chris Hellier/Corbis; **p.78** *l* © Fotomas/TopFoto, *c* © Hulton-Deutsch Collection/Corbis, *r* © Sean Sexton Collection/Corbis; **p.79** © Punch Ltd; **p.80** *r* © Bettmann/Corbis, *l* Punch; **p.81** Topfoto; **p.83** *Liam Neeson* © Lucy Nicholson/Reuters/Corbis, *Mary McAleese* Karl Schoendorfer/Rex Features, *Eamonn Holmes* Rex Features, *James Nesbitt* Rune Hellestad/Rex Features; **p.87** *t* © Toronto Public Library. Reproduced from the Toronto Public Library www.torontopubliclibrary.ca, *c* Archives of Ontario F 229-1-0-1, T Eaton Co fonds: Eaton's Catalogue Fall–Winter, 1884 front cover (reproduction 1978). Used with permission of Sears Canada Inc., *b* John Hasyn/First Light/Getty Images; **p.88** *t* Irish Linen Centre & Lisburn Museum Collection, *b* Private Collection/The Stapleton Collection/The Bridgeman Art Library; **p.89** © The Mariners' Museum/Corbis.

Acknowledgements **p.29** Liam Reilly for the extract from 'Flight of Earls'; **p.32** Bucks Music Group Limited and Tommy Makem for the lyrics from 'Four Green Fields'; **p.73** Pete St John for the lyrics from 'The Fields of Athenry'; **p.77** Dr Russell Rees.

Every effort has been made to trace all copyright holders, but if any have been inadvertently overlooked the Publishers will be pleased to make the necessary arrangements at the first opportunity.

Although every effort has been made to ensure that website addresses are correct at time of going to press, Hodder Education cannot be held responsible for the content of any website mentioned in this book. It is sometimes possible to find a relocated web page by typing in the address of the home page for a website in the URL window of your browser.

Hachette's policy is to use papers that are natural, renewable and recyclable products and made from wood grown in sustainable forests. The logging and manufacturing processes are expected to conform to the environmental regulations of the country of origin.

Orders: please contact Bookpoint Ltd, 130 Milton Park, Abingdon, Oxon OX14 4SB. Telephone: (44) 01235 827720. Fax: (44) 01235 400454. Lines are open 9.00–5.00, Monday to Saturday, with a 24-hour message answering service. Visit our website at www.hoddereducation.co.uk

© Sheelagh Dean, Cheryl Stafford and Catherine Thompson 2008
First published in 2008 by
Hodder Education, part of Hachette Livre UK
338 Euston Road
London NW1 3BH

Impression number   5 4 3 2 1
Year   2012 2011 2010 2009 2008

Cover photo: Nic Cleave Photography/Alamy
Illustrations by Oxford Designers and Illustrators and Richard Duszczak
Designed in Imperial BT by Fiona Webb
Printed in Italy

A catalogue record for this title is available from the British Library

ISBN: 978 0340 814 864

Contents

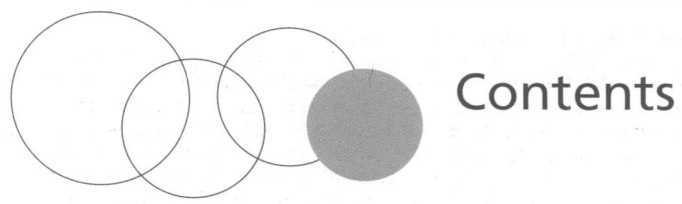

Your pathway through this book

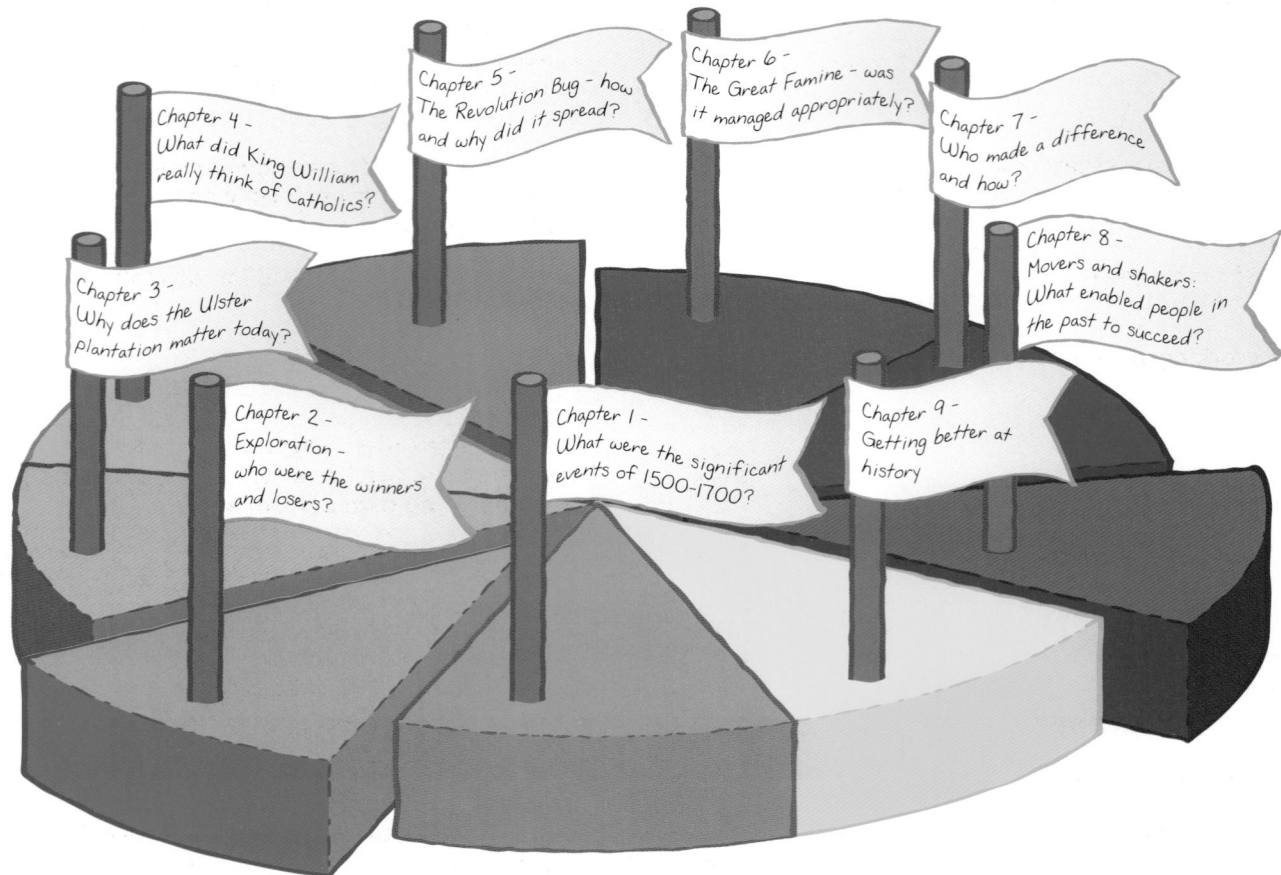

Chapter 4 – What did King William really think of Catholics?

Chapter 5 – The Revolution Bug – how and why did it spread?

Chapter 6 – The Great Famine – was it managed appropriately?

Chapter 7 – Who made a difference and how?

Chapter 8 – Movers and shakers: What enabled people in the past to succeed?

Chapter 3 – Why does the Ulster plantation matter today?

Chapter 2 – Exploration – who were the winners and losers?

Chapter 1 – What were the significant events of 1500–1700?

Chapter 9 – Getting better at history

As you make your way through this book you will start to develop the skills you need to be good at and enjoy history. The nine flags above show the chapter titles in the book, each of which asks a big question.

FEATURES OF THE BOOK

In Chapters 1–9 you will find:

● **Learning intentions**. These tell you the skills and knowledge you will be learning in the chapter.

● **Skills and capabilities icons**. These show you at a glance where you have the opportunity to develop some cross-curricular skills. These icons are explained in the table opposite.

● **Get Active.** These are tasks which help you improve your thinking and practise your skills in history.

● **Plan, Do, Review.** This helps you pull together all your work at the end of the chapter and gives you the opportunity to reflect on your own performance.

● **Key words**. These are highlighted in small capitals and are defined in a glossary at the back of the book.

The last chapter in the book, Chapter 9, asks you to reflect on all the skills you have developed throughout Year 9, and to use note-taking grids to help you practise these skills.

KEY ELEMENTS

Throughout your Key Stage 3 History course you will also study aspects of the past which help develop your understanding of the key elements of the curriculum, as shown in the table opposite. These are descriptions that will help you focus on the key messages of each chapter.

Skill/Capability	Icon	Description
Managing information		Research and manage information effectively to investigate historical issues, including identifying, collecting and using primary data and sources, and accessing and interpreting a range of secondary sources.
Thinking, problem-solving, decision-making		Show deeper historical understanding, be more critical, think flexibly and make reasoned judgments.
Being creative		Demonstrate creativity and initiative when developing own ideas.
Working with others		Work effectively with others.
Self-management		Demonstrate self-management by working systematically, persisting with tasks, evaluating and improving own performance.

Key element	Description
Personal understanding	Explore how history has affected your identity, culture and lifestyle.
Mutual understanding	Investigate how history has been selectively interpreted to create stereotypical perceptions and to justify views and actions.
Personal health	Investigate how and why health standards have changed over time.
Moral character	Investigate individuals who are considered to have taken a significant moral stand and examine their motivation and legacy.
Spiritual awareness	Investigate and evaluate the spiritual beliefs and legacy of civilisations.
Citizenship	Investigate the long- and short-term causes and consequences of the partition of Ireland and how it has influenced Northern Ireland today, including key events and turning points.
Cultural understanding	Investigate the impact of significant events and ideas of the twentieth century on the world.
Media awareness	Critically investigate and evaluate the power of the media in their representation of a significant, historical event or individual.
Ethical awareness	Investigate ethical issues in history or historical figures who have behaved ethically or unethically.
Employability	Investigate how the skills developed through history will be useful in a range of careers, and the characteristics and achievements of entrepreneurs over time.
Economic awareness	Investigate the changing nature of local and global economies over time, and the impact of technology in the workplace over time.
Education for sustainable development	Investigate the need to preserve history in the local and global environment and evaluate the environmental impact of wars, Industrial Revolution, etc.

Introduction: What changes happened during 1500–1900?

GET ACTIVE 1

a Look at the pictures in the timeline below. They represent some of the topics you will be learning about in Year 9. Make a list of the topics you think they represent.

b Now make a list of any questions you have about these topics. When thinking about which questions to ask, remember to use the 5W approach you learned about in Year 8: What? When? Why? Who? Where?

In this book you will be investigating how life changed for people living in Ireland, Europe and other parts of the world during the period 1500–1900. It was a time of great changes in religion, society, trade, how countries were ruled and also how people's ideas changed about the world in which they lived. Many of the changes that took place in this period have helped shape the world in which we live today. Here are some of the changes that took place:

- PARLIAMENT became more important;
- Europe became divided by religion;
- Britain gained a huge overseas EMPIRE;
- Ireland and England became one country by the ACT OF UNION 1801;
- INDUSTRIAL REVOLUTION began in England.

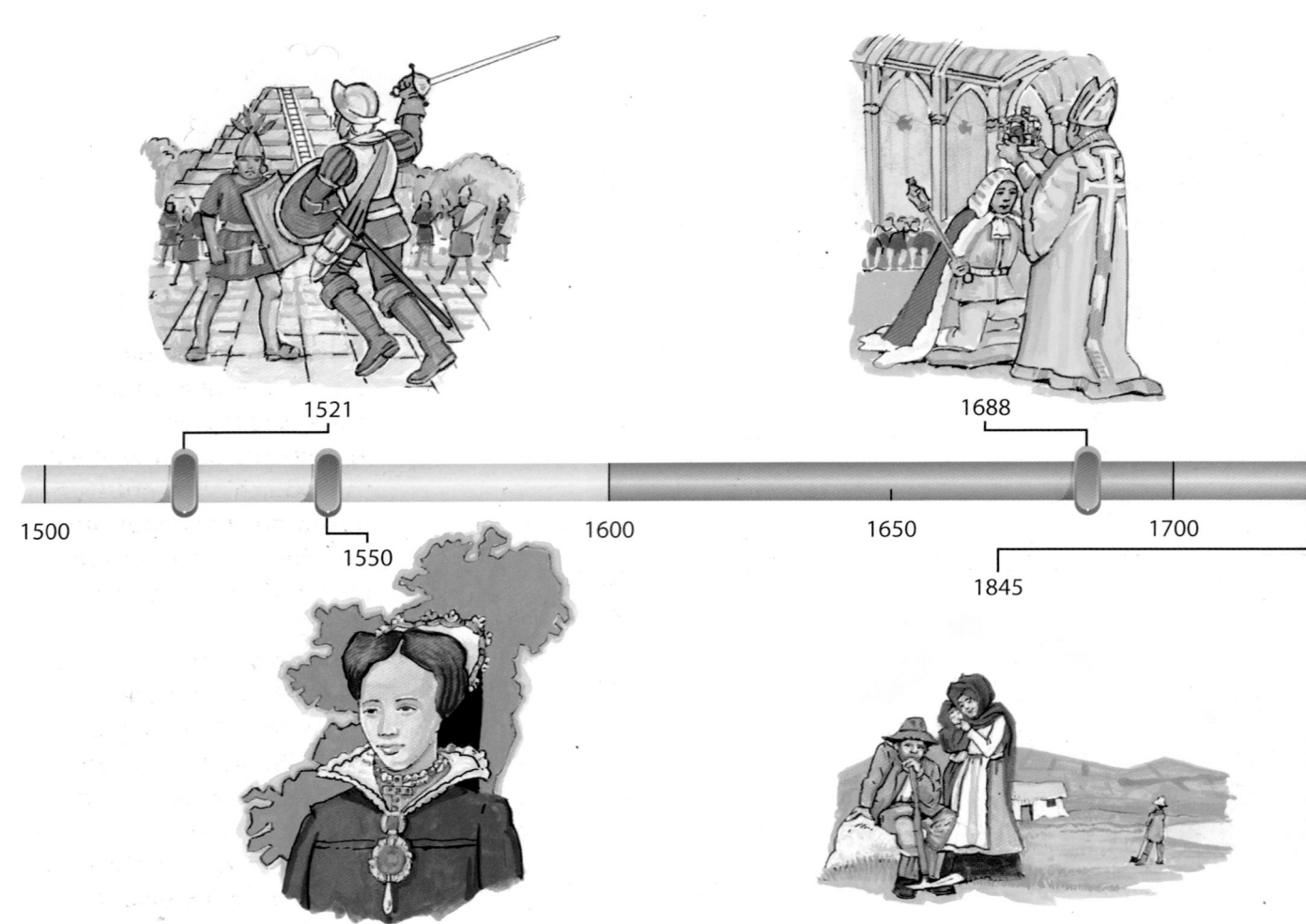

1521

1688

1500   1600   1650   1700

1550

1845

Ever heard the word?

In Year 9, you will be introduced to a lot of new terms or names. Some you may have heard before but don't know the meaning of. Copy and complete the grid below and see how many new words you will have to learn.

Word	Never heard it	Heard it but don't know what it means	Can write what the word means
Renaissance			
Reformation			
Plantation			
Invention			
Colony			
Revolution			
Parliament			

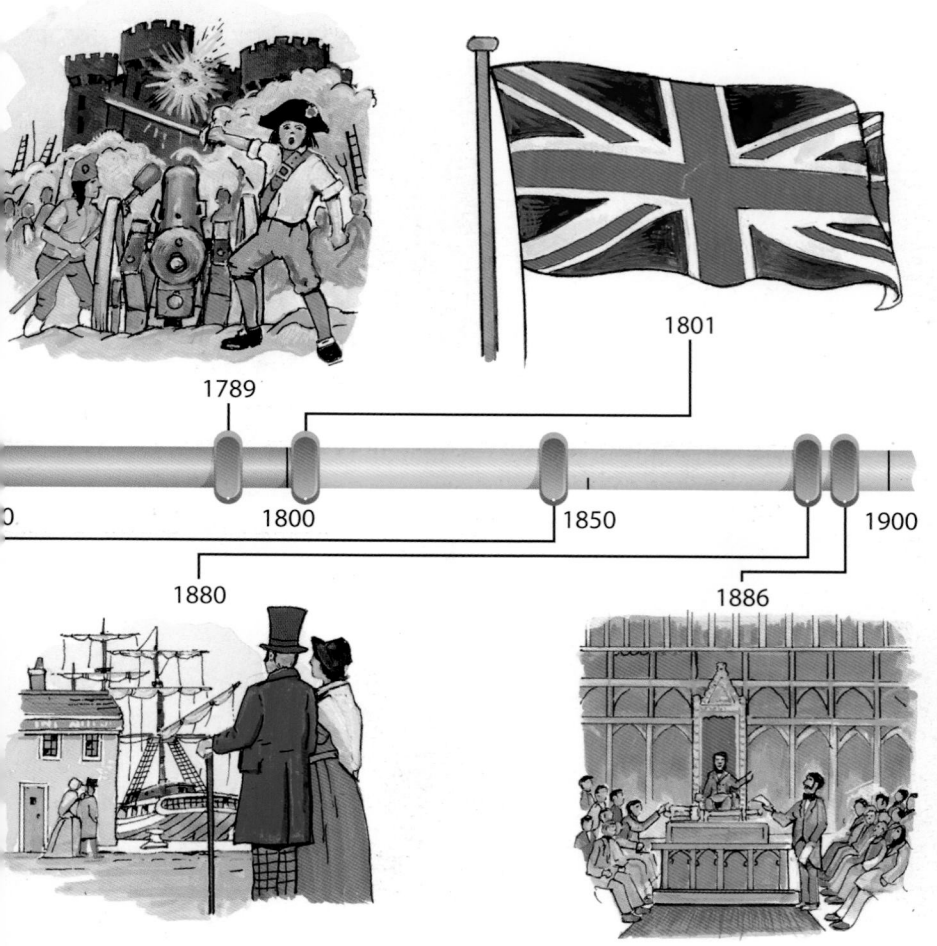

1789
1801
1800
1850
1900
1880
1886

GET ACTIVE 2

a Look at the timeline. Choose one event that looks exciting or interesting, and one event that you think might turn out to be very important. Are the events you have chosen different or the same?

b If the two events you chose in part a were different, which do you think should be studied? Do you think we should study just the most exciting events in history, or the most important ones?

1 What were the significant events of 1500–1700?

In this chapter we are learning to:
- ✓ understand what the term significance is;
- ✓ know what was significant about the period 1500–1700;
- ✓ use criteria to assess the significance of events and people in the period;
- ✓ select and organise relevant and important information.

Have you ever wondered why you remember some topics you studied in history and not others? Or how we decide what makes a topic important enough to study in history? If you had to choose which topics you could study in Year 9, I wonder if they would be the same ones that have been chosen for this book. What makes something important in history and worthy of study is called SIGNIFICANCE. Let's begin by looking at what events you think are important and why.

36,000 people left homeless during July floods in 2007.

Northern Ireland born football legend George Best dies in 2005.

Last Harry Potter book launched in July 2007.

The execution of Saddam Hussein in 2006.

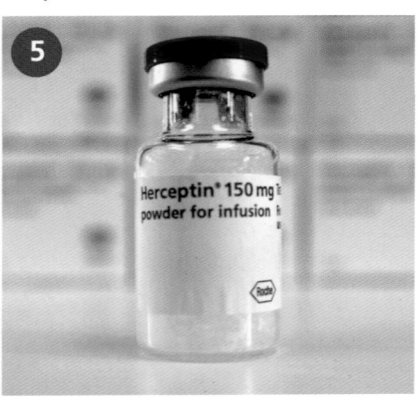

Scientists discover new cancer drug Herceptin in 2006.

Portable media player, the iPod, launched in 2001.

GET ACTIVE 1

Which of the six events are important, and why?

a Get a partner and look at the six events. What do you notice about the events, e.g. things they have in common, or how they are different? Would any of the events be well known around the world? Have all the events happened in your lifetime?
Write down your first thoughts and share your findings with the rest of the class.

b Match each event to one of the words below:
war, technology, medicine, disaster, entertainment, sport.
Write down which of the events are local, national and international.

c Your next task is to decide which of the events you think was the most important, and why. Use the Priority Pyramid on the right to help you record your answer by putting the most important reason at the top.

Explain your answer to the class and be ready to justify your choices.

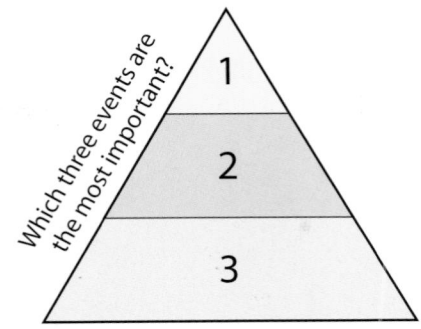

Which are the three most important events?

GET ACTIVE 2

Are some events more significant than others, and how do we decide?

a Below is a list of points that make some events significant in history. These points are called CRITERIA. Complete the table below using the six events.

Reasons for being significant	Name of event
It affected a lot of people.	
It changed people's lives forever.	
It tells us what was happening to people at a particular time.	
If it hadn't happened, then things might have turned out differently.	
It tells us something about our world today.	
It affected a lot of people deeply.	

b Share your findings with the other groups in the class. What do you notice about how others made their decisions? Why would there be these differences?

WHICH WERE THE MOST SIGNIFICANT EVENTS IN 1500–1700?

People living during 1500–1700 experienced great changes. Many historians call this time the Early Modern Age, because some of the changes that happened then still affect our world today. In this section, we will look at what you think are the most important events in a period of history.

1500–1700 What happened when?

In 1500 Italy was the centre of art, culture and new ideas about the world and how it worked. These ideas led to a movement called the RENAISSANCE, and a new way of thinking developed where scholars began to rely less on what the Church told them and to work things out for themselves.

Some of the most famous artists and sculptors lived at this time, e.g. Michelangelo (1475–1564), Raphael (1486–1520) and Leonardo Da Vinci (1452–1519) who painted the 'Mona Lisa'.

In 1534 Henry VIII, King of England, started the Protestant religion in England and Ireland by breaking away from the Catholic Church so that he could remarry and get a son.

Mary Tudor, Queen of England 1553–4, used a new way of controlling Ireland called PLANTATIONS. The first one was in Laois and the second in Offaly.

In 1517 a German monk called Martin Luther began an important movement called the REFORMATION, during which he quarrelled with the Pope and set up his own Protestant Church.

There were many well-known Elizabethans. William Shakespeare was the most famous English playwright ever (1564–1616), and 400 years after his death his plays are still performed in theatres all over the world. In 1581 Sir Francis Drake was the first English man to sail around the world, and earned himself the reputation of the greatest EXPLORER of the age.

The printing press had been invented in 1450 by Johannes Gutenburg, so by 1500 more people were learning to read and write and find out about new ideas. In 1571 the first book was printed in Ireland in Gaelic.

There were great developments in science. Galileo was a famous astronomer (1564–1642) who used the telescope to observe the skies, and proved that the earth and planets went round the sun. Sir Isaac Newton (1642–1727) discovered the law of gravity, which helped to explain why the planets are held together in the solar system as they moved around the sun. He was voted most important scientist ever in a 2005 poll of scientists.

More exploration led to more wars, and England and Spain fought over the treasure coming from the new world. In 1577 Spain sent a huge fleet of ships called the ARMADA to attack England, but it failed and many of the Spanish ships were shipwrecked off the west coast of Ireland on their way back to Spain.

Ever since sugar was exported to England in the sixteenth century from COLONIES overseas, we have been able to use it in desserts or sweet courses as part of our meals.

After the execution of King Charles I by PARLIAMENT in 1649, the monarchy was abolished and a COMMONWEALTH established.

In 1691, the PENAL LAWS were passed in Ireland against two groups of people who did not attend the new Protestant Church – the Catholics and PRESBYTERIANS. These laws prevented them from certain jobs, having the vote and owning land. These laws eventually helped to create a new ruling group in Ireland known as the PROTESTANT ASCENDANCY.

Some of the most famous kings and queens in history ruled at this time:
Henry VIII 1509–47, Elizabeth I 1558–1603, James II 1685–8, and William of Orange 1689–1702.

The first stock exchange grew out of the coffee houses of seventeenth-century London, and the earliest evidence of organised trading was in 1698.

GET ACTIVE 3

a Sort the events in the timeline into:

- important inventions and discoveries;
- important people;
- important changes.

Some entries may apply to more than one section. What do you notice about this period? Do you think it was an important time to live?

b Match each of the events on the timeline with the explanations below that historians have come up with to help them decide why past events are important.

- This event affected the lives of many people in the past.
- Things would have been different if this event had not happened.
- This helps us to explain something about our world today.
- This event affected people's lives for a long time.
- This event tells us how people lived in the past.

c Which three events do you think are the most important, and why? Compare your answers with the rest of the class and note any differences in the choices other people have made. Can you give any reasons for the differences?

WHAT MAKES PEOPLE IN THE PAST SIGNIFICANT?

In the last section you looked at what made some events more important than others during 1500–1700. Now we will look at what made a person from that time significant.

HENRY VIII – FAMOUS, INFAMOUS OR SIGNIFICANT?

1. Catherine of Aragon 1509–1533 divorced.

2. Anne Boleyn 1533–1536 executed.

3. Jane Seymour 1536–1537 died.

4. Anne of Cleves 1540 divorced.

5. Catherine Howard 1540–1542 executed.

6. Catherine Parr widowed 1547.

Henry VIII is one of the most famous kings in British history, and if you opened any history textbook on this period he will certainly be written about. What is it about this king that has made him the subject of so many films, plays, books and operas? First, let's see who he was and what he was famous for.

Henry was born into the Tudor family who ruled England from 1485 to 1603. When his father Henry married his mother Elizabeth of York, the marriage put an end to 30 years of war between the two families. Henry was the second son and was expected to have a career in the church. When Arthur died in 1502, Henry (aged 11) was heir to the throne and had to marry Arthur's wife, a Spanish princess called Catherine of Aragon.

1 A powerful king

This portrait of Henry VIII in 1539, when he was 46 years old, was painted by a famous painter called Hans Holbein.

2 An accomplished prince

'His Majesty is the handsomest POTENTATE I ever set eyes on; above the usual height, with an extremely fine calf to his leg, his complexion very fair and bright, with auburn hair combed straight and short, in the French fashion, his throat being rather long and thick. He speaks French, English, and Latin, and a little Italian, plays well on the lute and harpsichord, sings from books at sight, draws the bow with greater strength than any man in England, and JOUSTS marvellously. Believe me, he is in every respect a most accomplished Prince.'

A contemporary description

Painting of Henry VIII playing the harp.

3 A cruel tyrant

Henry executed anyone who opposed him, including one of his own ministers, Thomas Cromwell, in 1540. He executed Thomas More in 1536, a leading Catholic spokesman and philosopher who dared to criticise him. This gave him a reputation as a cruel TYRANT.

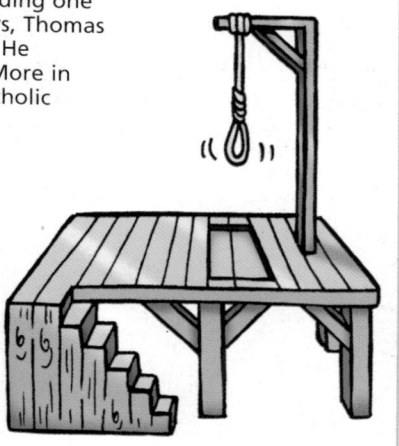

4 The divided church

When Henry became king, the country was Catholic and was controlled by the Pope in Rome. When the Pope refused to let Henry have a divorce from his first wife, Henry made himself head of the Church of England instead and gave himself the divorce he wanted. This started the event called the English Reformation.

5 Founder of the navy

Henry established the English navy and had many ships built to protect England and stop foreign invasions.

The *Mary Rose*.

6 A ruthless king

He decided to close down 376 monasteries because he needed their wealth to help finance his wars and to set up the new religion. In 1536, he ruthlessly put down a rebellion of people who protested against the closure of the monasteries, called the Pilgrimage of Grace. He forced the new religion on Ireland, and made the Gaelic lords attend Parliament for the first time. He also got himself declared King of Ireland in 1541.

Mellifont Abbey, 1539.

7 A spendthrift

When Henry came to the throne he was king of one of the richest countries in Europe. When he died in 1547 he had spent so much money on wars with France and Scotland, paintings and palaces that England was bankrupt.

8 Six wives, two daughters and one son

Between 1507 and 1547 Henry married six times. He divorced his first wife, Catherine, because she was only able to give him a daughter, Mary. He then married Anne Boleyn, who gave him a second daughter, Elizabeth, in 1533, but he had her beheaded when he found out she was unfaithful. His third wife, Jane Seymour, gave him his son Edward, but she died soon after childbirth. He then married a German princess, Anne of Cleves, but the marriage did not last long and he soon divorced her. Catherine Howard, who was only a teenager when they got married in 1540, was also beheaded because she was unfaithful. His final wife was Catherine Parr, whom he was married to from 1543 until his death in 1547.

GET ACTIVE 4

a Read the accounts (1–8) of Henry VIII's life. What aspects would make him an interesting topic to study in school? Make a list of five interesting facts and then share them with the rest of the class.

b Was Henry VIII really that significant? Here are some of the long-term effects of Henry's reign, which explain why Henry might be considered significant in history. Read the six explanation cards and then choose the three you think are the most important. Give reasons why.

He encouraged the development of geographical exploration, which in the reign of his daughter Elizabeth gave England a worldwide reputation.

Kings and queens after him were strong and powerful.

The Catholic Church in England was divided, and there followed a long period of RELIGIOUS PERSECUTION where both Protestants and Catholics were killed because of their religion.

Henry remained Catholic until he died, despite having started the Protestant religion in England in 1534.

Many people felt bitter for a long time about the closure of the monasteries, because there was nowhere else that poor people could get help.

By challenging the authority of the Pope, Henry was saying he was head of state and wanted to control his own country.

THE SIGNIFICANCE OF STUDYING HISTORY

When you study why events and people are important in history, you are practising an important life skill – the ability to make informed decisions. Being able to pick out the most important points about a topic or problem and knowing why they are important is a skill you can practise in other subjects.

When you apply for jobs later in your life, you will be given a set of criteria which tell you what the employer is looking for. History will develop that same skill of using criteria to help you come up with answers and solutions to situations in life where you have to make a decision.

Plan, Do, Review

In this chapter you have worked through which events you think are significant in your own lives, and looked at the criteria which would help historians to assess the significance of events, individuals or themes in history. Now we shall pull together your ideas with those of historians to summarise why things are significant in history.

PLAN

Look back through your work in this chapter. You need to look at the reasons you gave for why events are important to you, and the reasons historians gave for events being important. The grid below will help you to gather your information.

My reasons for thinking things are important	Historians' reasons for thinking things are important

1 Make a list of your reasons.
2 Make a list of historians' reasons.
3 Add on any other reasons you may have picked up from your own research. Think about what significant events in history tell us about ourselves.

DO

Copy the Venn diagram into your book.

- Inside the blue circle put the title 'My Choice' and write words or phrases which best explain your reasons for significance.
- Inside the yellow circle write the title 'What Historians Think' and then add the words and phrases that best explain historians' reasons.
- Inside the middle green section now fill in words or phrases that are common to both you and the historians.

REVIEW

- Think about and record in green ink why you think using the Venn diagram to record your ideas was useful.
- Write down in amber or orange how you could use the diagram in other areas of history or other subjects.
- Write down in red one way in which you might have recorded your ideas differently and why.

2 Exploration – who were the winners and losers?

In this chapter we are learning to:
- ✓ weigh up pros and cons of exploration on societies in the past;
- ✓ identify a range of different factors for a development in the past;
- ✓ manage information in the form of a piece of discursive writing.

Have you ever gone exploring? It can be an exciting yet slightly scary experience. Today, there are different types of exploration. For example, exploration around the world, exploration in science, and entrepreneurs who explore new business ideas.

GET ACTIVE 1

a Look at the three lines of pictures on the right, and in each line decide which item is the odd one out. Give reasons for your choices.

b In pairs, discuss the following questions; you could use the odd one out examples to help you.

- What are the benefits of exploration to society?
- What can we learn from EXPLORERS?

c Now share your ideas in fours, come up with your five best points, and feed these back to the class.

1	Spaceman	Internet explorer	Satellite
2	Businessman	Inventor	Entrepreneur
3	Sea explorer	Mountain explorer	Arctic explorer

WHAT MOTIVATES AN EXPLORER?

Throughout history, people have been on the move. In Year 8, you found out about the different people who came to Ireland in the past. In this chapter, we are going to investigate why people from Europe in the fifteenth and sixteenth centuries went exploring around the world. What could be won when people went to new lands and what could be lost when they went there?

Bartholomew Diaz discovered the southern tip of Africa in 1488.

Christopher Columbus discovered the 'new world' of the Americas in 1492.

Vasco da Gama sailed past the southern tip of Africa and reached India in 1498.

Ferdinand Magellan was the first person to sail around the world, 1519–22. His journey began to question the idea that the earth was flat.

Have you ever thought about how people made money in the past? In the fifteenth and sixteenth centuries, European countries became rich through TRADE. Ships went to far-off lands such as China to find goods to bring back like sugar, spices and cloth. The race to find new land had begun, and explorers were eager to seek out new lands in order to gain more opportunities for trade. So, economic reasons encouraged people to go exploring. Many explorers were poor men who did not own land and could not find jobs at home. They went exploring to find money and fame. Rich people were willing to invest in the voyages, as they thought they could make money from the discovery of new lands and from trade.

There were also political reasons for exploration. The richer a country became through trade, the more powerful it could become. Kings and queens were willing to support voyages of discovery in order to increase the power of their country. Land meant power. The race to find new land led to the setting up of COLONIES. People from European countries went and lived in these colonies in the new world.

Finally, there were religious reasons for exploration. Some explorers like Prince Henry of Portugal wanted to spread Christian beliefs in the new world.

GET ACTIVE 2

a Who explored where? Use your research skills to find out about different explorers. Here is a grid for you to copy, to help you record your information.

Name of explorer	Date	Place explored

b In groups, choose an explorer. Using the internet, books and your library, try to collect information about that person in order to answer the following questions:

- What motivated that person to go exploring? Why did they go? What did they hope to achieve?
- What types of skills do you think the explorer needed to do their job well?
- What obstacles did the explorer face?
- How did they overcome the obstacles?

c Draw an outline of a person and label it with the name of the explorer you have chosen. Then record your answers from part b around it. You might like to include words like planning, fund-raising, leading others, persevering when things got tough …

WHAT WERE THE EFFECTS OF EXPLORATION?

Were there any benefits for the native people in welcoming the explorers?

The first contact between the native people and the explorers usually involved the exchange of gifts. The native people might give furs and in return the explorers would give mirrors, beads, rings, axes, knives, blankets and kettles. The native people found these goods very interesting and began to call the newcomers 'the iron people' or the 'cloth makers'.

How has the Spanish conquest of Mexico been portrayed?

When Christopher Columbus crossed the Atlantic in 1492 and discovered the Caribbean islands, he was looking for the Indies, and so he called the native people 'Indians'. The new land he discovered was known as 'New Spain'. In 1519, a Spanish explorer Hernando CORTES set out to take over the land that is now Mexico by conquering the Aztec people. The Spanish realised that the wealth of these lands of 'New Spain' would make them rich. The Spanish also set out to convert the native people to Christianity. We are going to investigate what was won and lost during the Spanish conquest of Mexico by looking at how these events have been portrayed in history.

SOURCE 1

A caricature of Cortes and his men painted by Diego Rivera (1886–1957) who was a **Mexican painter and REVOLUTIONARY.**

SOURCE 2

The Spaniards with their horses, their spears and lances, began to commit murders and other strange cruelties. They entered into towns and villages, sparing neither children nor old men and women. They ripped their bellies and cut them to pieces as if they had been slaughtering lambs in a field. They made bets with each other over who could thrust a sword into the middle of a man or who could cut off his head with one stroke. They took little ones by their heels and crushed their heads against the cliffs. Others they threw into the rivers laughing and mocking them as they tumbled into the water. They put everyone they met to death.

One time I saw four or five important native nobles roasted on makeshift grills. They cried out pitifully. This thing troubled our Captain that he could not sleep. He commanded that they be strangled. The Sergeant … would not strangle them but put bullets into their mouths instead.

I have seen all these things and others. Most tried to flee. They tried to hide in the mountains. They tried to flee from these men. Men who were empty of all pity, behaved like savage beasts. They are nothing more than slaughterers and enemies of mankind. These evil men had even taught their hounds, fierce dogs, to tear natives to pieces at first sight.

And, when, although rare, the Indians put to death some Spaniards, the Spaniards made an agreement that for every one Spaniard killed they had to kill one hundred Indians.

Once the Indians came to meet us bringing food and good cheer! Instead, the devil, which had put himself in the Spaniards, killed them all in my presence, without any cause whatsoever, more than three thousand souls. I saw there such great cruelties, that never any man living either have or shall see the like.

In three or four months (myself being present) there died more than six thousand children, which the Spanish had sent into the gold mines.

This account is from Bartolomé de Las Casas written in c.1513. He was a missionary priest and became the first Bishop of Chiapas in Mexico.

GET ACTIVE 3

Source 1 is a painting which was painted a long time after the Spanish conquest. Source 2 was written at the time of the events by a Spanish priest who had come with the conquistadors to 'New Spain'.

a Look carefully at Source 1. In pairs, make a list of all the things that you can see in the painting.

b Try to decide what message the artist is trying to give. What is the artist's viewpoint about the Spanish Conquest of 'New Spain' in the Americas?

c In what ways does Source 2 support Source 1?

d Are there any differences between Sources 1 and 2?

GET ACTIVE 4

a You are going to have a silent conversation around Source 2. This means that your teacher will give you a copy of the source on a big piece of paper. You will work in pairs, reading the source very carefully. Have one pen between you, and as you read the source circle key words or write comments about things in the wording that shock you, or a question you'd like to ask. In your pairs have a silent conversation – see if you can remain silent and only communicate by writing on the big paper.

b Think about:

- What was happening to the native people?
- What did the author think about his fellow Spanish?
- What words did he use to describe them?
- How were the Spanish portrayed?
- What reasons are you given for their actions? Are they justified?
- What shocks you in this source?

c What human rights were being infringed?

d What does this source show about the loss for the native people? What did the Spanish gain? Did they lose anything?

MYSTERY: WHAT HAPPENED TO THE SETTLERS IN ROANOKE IN 1587?

SOURCE 3

At our first coming to anchor on this shore we saw a great smoke rise in the isle of Roanoke near the place where I left our colony in the year 1587, this put us in good hope that some of the colony was expecting us. And so we passed toward the place where we left them, in 1585, in houses, but we found the houses taken down and the place was strongly enclosed with a high palisade of trees. On one of the posts of the fort, the word CROATOAN was engraved into the post. We found the grass and rotten trees burning around the place. From there we went along by the waterside toward the point of the creek to see if we could find any of their boats, but we could see no sign of them nor any of the small guns which were left with them on my departure. At our return from the creek some of our sailors meeting us told us that they had found bodies and human remains.

This is an extract from an account by John White who visited the English colony at Roanoke in North America in 1590. John White had left his daughter, Eleanor Dare, and his son-in-law, Annanias Dare. Eleanor had given birth to a daughter, Virginia. John White never saw his family again.

When you investigated the Spanish conquest of Mexico, you explored what was lost by the native people and how the Spanish gained the land. In history, however, the winners can also be losers. You are going to see how some conquerors or settlers did not always win.

Just as the Spanish were conquering lands in Central and South America, their rivals the English wanted to gain land in the new world. In 1584, a small expedition went to the new world to explore the land. They went to Roanoke Island and met with the Roanoke tribe. A third expedition left England in May 1587. In March 1588, reports had reached England that supplies were low in the colony in Roanoke and the Indians were hostile. It was planned to send ships to help the colony but the Spanish ARMADA appeared off the coast of England and all ships were needed to prevent the Spanish from taking over England. Read Source 3 to see what John White found when he eventually returned to the colony at Roanoke in 1590.

A nineteenth-century engraving which shows John White returning to Roanoke Island in 1590.

GET ACTIVE 5

In history, we explore reasons for events. You are going to think about why the settlers disappeared at Roanoke in 1590.

a Look at the factors (in the boxes) that could be given to explain the disappearance of the settlers in Roanoke in North America by 1587. Try to categorise them into which ones are:

- irrelevant;
- partly relevant;
- very relevant.

b In pairs, decide what you think is the best explanation and put forward a hypothesis about what happened to the settlers. A hypothesis is a theory or an idea that you use to explain something or why something happened.

c Listen to the different hypotheses around your class.

- Which ones are convincing? Why?
- Which ones are less convincing? Why?

d Write an explanation after listening to your class discussion to explain what you think happened to the settlers of Roanoke in 1587.

e Use the internet to find some explanations given by historians about what happened at Roanoke. Compare your explanation with some of the explanations given by historians.

> The settlers found it difficult to grow crops and grew hungry. Hunger led to death.

> Many settlers caught diseases like malaria and typhoid.

> The settlers fell out amongst themselves and started fighting each other.

> When John White visited Roanoke in 1590 the settlers were on holiday.

> The native people (Native American Indians) were angry at the white people for taking their land, so they attacked the settlers.

> The settlers got bored and decided to go somewhere else.

> Many settlers did not like living at Roanoke and so decided to go back to England to live.

> The settlers made friends with the native people and decided to go and live with them. The native people were nomadic, which meant they moved to different places during the year.

> The settlers were playing a game of hide and seek with John White when he visited them.

> The settlers had to work very hard to keep their settlement going. Many of them died of exhaustion.

> The settlers were abducted by aliens.

> The Spanish came and attacked the English settlers because they were enemies at the time. The Spanish did not want any other Europeans taking over land in the new world.

> The word Croatan was a secret code word for where the settlers had gone.

WHY DID THE PILGRIM FATHERS NOT HEED THE WARNING OF ROANOKE AND JAMESTOWN?

SOURCE 4

There were never Englishmen left in a foreign country in such misery as we were in this new discovered Virginia. We watched every three nights, lying on the bare cold ground, what weather so ever came; guarded all the next day; which brought our men to be the most feeble wretches, not having five able men to man our defences.

From Captain John Smith and Virginia (Then and There series, Longman 1968)

Have you seen the film *Pocahontas*? It depicts the story of the settlers from England who went to America in 1607. This was another attempt at setting up a colony by England after the disappearance of the settlers at Roanoke. King James I allowed the London Virginia company to establish a colony in Virginia, America. The colony was called Jamestown, and was England's first colony in America. One of the first settlers was Captain John Smith. By September 1607, however, half of the original 104 settlers were dead from disease and the settlers had come under attack from the Native American Indians.

SOURCE 5

This is a European artist's impression of the massacre of settlers at Martin's Hundred in 1622. This gives us an impression of the dangers that the settlers faced and the complete surprise on their faces when they were attacked by the native people.

Despite these warnings more settlers went to America in 1620. They were known as the PILGRIM FATHERS. Many were PURITANS who wanted to leave England to set up a 'New England' where they could have their own church and be free to practise their religion. Some of the settlers were not Puritans but hoped to make their fortune. Over half of the settlers died in their first year. Despite this, between 1630 and 1641, 22,000 migrants travelled to America.

GET ACTIVE 6

What do Sources 4 and 5 show about the experiences of the early settlers?

GET ACTIVE 7

Throughout this chapter you have been looking at why people were prepared to move in the fifteenth and sixteenth centuries. The reasons can be divided into push and pull factors: a push factor is something in your own circumstances that pushes you to do something; a pull factor is something that draws you to do something new.

a What were the push and pull factors that encouraged people to move in the fifteenth and sixteenth centuries?

b Why do people move today? Make a list of push and pull factors.

c Is your list similar or different to the one you did in part a?

Despite the harsh conditions that many of the settlers had to face in the new world, exploration continued and countries established colonies. The map below shows the extent of colonisation in the sixteenth century. Later on, this colonisation would spread to Africa and Asia.

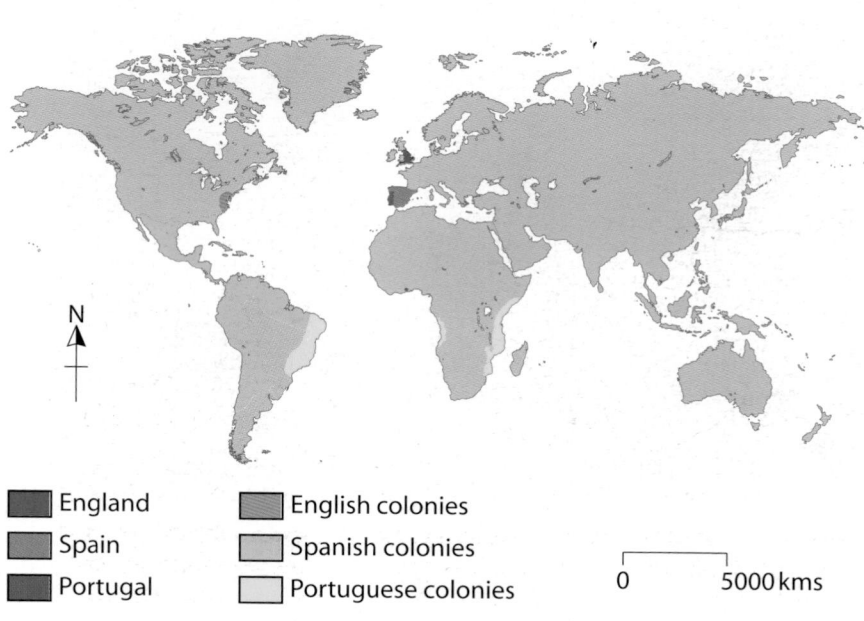

England   English colonies
Spain   Spanish colonies
Portugal   Portuguese colonies

0   5000 kms

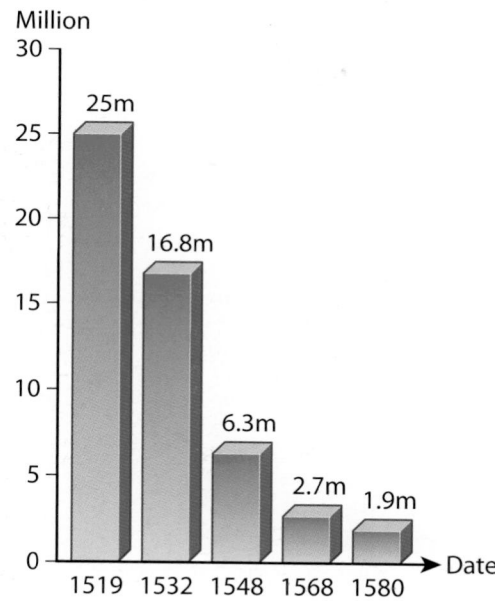

The decline of the native population of New Spain in the sixteenth century.

It is important to consider the impact of colonisation on the native people. For example, the graph on the right shows a decline in the native population of New Spain in the sixteenth century. Many native people died of overwork and cruelty. The Europeans brought with them diseases which killed many native people.

GET ACTIVE 8

a What does the graph show?

b What factors explain the changes in the population of the native people?

Plan, Do, Review

EXPLORATION – WHO WERE THE WINNERS AND LOSERS?

In this chapter you have found out why exploration developed from the fifteenth century and the experiences of the settlers and native people. You have been considering why people went exploring and who were the winners and losers as a result of the expeditions. Your task is to write a piece of DISCURSIVE WRITING. This is a piece of writing which looks at both sides of an argument.

PLAN

Stage 1

Read carefully through this chapter. You need to look at the evidence and see in what ways the native people gained or lost during this period. Likewise, in what ways did the explorers and settlers gain or lose during the period? Here is a grid to help you record your information:

Type of person	Plus points	Minus points
Native people – these were the people who lived in the land before the settlers arrived		
Settlers – these were the people who came to settle in the new lands in order to trade goods		

- List all the reasons in this chapter that show exploration as beneficial to either group.
- List all the reasons in this chapter that show exploration as not beneficial to either group. Who suffered as a result of the exploration?
- You could research other examples from history and life today to strengthen your argument.

Stage 2

Introduction: It is important to begin your piece of discursive writing with an introduction. This is where you explain the issue to be addressed, i.e. the two sides to the argument for the two parties: in what ways the explorers won and lost during their expeditions, and in what ways the native people won and lost during the age of exploration.

Paragraph 1: You could begin by looking at the benefits to the explorers, e.g. *on the one hand it could be suggested that the explorers were the winners in exploration because ...*
You will then need to provide reasons and evidence for this side of the argument.

Paragraph 2: Now you can consider the damage to the explorers, e.g. *on the other hand, it could be argued that at times the explorers or settlers were the losers because ...*
You will then need to provide reasons and evidence for this side of the argument.

Paragraph 3: Now you can consider any benefits to the native people, e.g. *on the one hand it could be suggested that the native people were the winners in the age of exploration because ...*
You will then need to provide reasons and evidence for this side of the argument.

Paragraph 4: And finally you can consider the damage to the native people, e.g. *on the other hand it could be suggested that the native people were the losers in the age of exploration because ...*
You will then need to provide reasons and evidence for this side of the argument.

Conclusion: In the conclusion you reach a judgment in response to the question. For example,
Having considered who were the winners and losers during the age of exploration, I think ... because ...

DO

Write your piece of discursive writing. Get a partner to read it in order to make sure all the points make sense. Read over your work carefully to make sure there are no errors. Check for spelling mistakes, punctuation and clear meaning.

REVIEW

Think about and record:

- Three things you learned from this investigation and from writing a piece of discursive writing.
- Two things you would do differently if you were to produce a piece of discursive writing again.
- One question that you still have about the issue of exploration.

3 Why does the Ulster plantation matter today?

In this chapter we are learning to:
- ✓ recognise the impact of the Ulster plantation on life today in Northern Ireland;
- ✓ investigate how history has been used to create stereotypical views in Northern Ireland;
- ✓ work with others to create a multimedia presentation.

Just as people were on the move exploring the new world, let's investigate why settlers came to Ireland in the sixteenth and seventeenth centuries. As you learned in Year 8, the Normans came to take over Ireland in 1169. By the early fifteenth century, English power had declined in Ireland. Most of the land was controlled by Irish Gaelic chieftains. England began to get frightened that Ireland could be used as a base by the enemies of England to launch an attack.

What do you remember about King Henry VIII? He wanted to have stricter control over Ireland. Henry VIII used a range of different methods of control.

Henry VIII, King of England 1509–47.

- Firstly, he sent troops to crush rebellions in Ireland.
- Then he appointed his own Englishmen to important jobs ruling Ireland, because he felt they would be more loyal to him than Irishmen.
- In 1536, Henry declared himself the Head of the Church of England. Henry made Protestantism the official religion in Ireland. Catholicism was banned and land belonging to the Catholic Church was CONFISCATED.
- Fourthly, in 1541 Henry called himself 'King of Ireland'.
- Finally, Henry used a policy of 'surrender and regrant' to control the Gaelic lords. The Gaelic chiefs were encouraged to surrender their lands to the King but were given them back if they swore loyalty to Henry.

During the reign of Mary Tudor (1553–8), settlers were encouraged to go to Ireland by being given land. In return for the land, settlers had to build stone houses and keep arms for their protection. This example of PLANTATION did not succeed because not enough settlers wanted to go to Ireland.

Mary Tudor, Queen of England 1553–8.

During the reign of Elizabeth I (1558–1603), there were rebellions in Ireland. When troops sent from England stopped these rebellions, a plantation began in Munster in 1586. A plantation was when settlers were encouraged to go to Ireland by being granted land. When they were there, they would rule the land they owned and remain loyal to Queen Elizabeth I. These settlers could help Elizabeth to control the Irish people. However, the attacks by the Irish made life difficult and dangerous for the settlers. Most of them left Ireland by 1600. War broke out between the English and Irish in 1593. The English were defeated at Clontibret in 1595 and at Yellow Ford in 1598. In order to regain control, the English began to burn land, which meant the Irish people starved. The Irish under the leadership of Hugh O'Neill, Earl of Tyrone were defeated at the Battle of Kinsale in 1601. O'Neill surrendered in 1603.

Elizabeth I, Queen of England 1558–1603.

GET ACTIVE 1

a List the methods that the Tudor king and queens used to try to keep stricter control of Ireland. Then prioritise your list with the most effective method at the top and the least effective at the bottom.

b Mary I and Elizabeth I used a policy of plantation to try to control Ireland. Think about the process of planting something and explain what they were hoping to achieve.

c Suppose you are an adviser to the new King of England and Scotland, James I, who has become king in 1603. You have to give him a report about the situation in Ireland. You are going to use the layout of a SWOT analysis. Think about the 'strengths' of the English crown in Ireland, some of the 'weaknesses', the 'opportunities' to be gained in Ireland but also some of the 'threats' or difficulties to be faced in trying to gain stricter control of Ireland.

GET ACTIVE 2

In pairs, you are going to complete two living graphs by copying and completing the graph below.

a Firstly, consider the events which happened in the dates on the graph, from the position of either Henry VIII, Mary or Elizabeth. Plot on the graph whether the English crown and government would be happy or unhappy with events. Label your living graph – from the viewpoint of the English crown.

b Then complete a living graph as a native Irish person reflecting on the impact of the events in Ireland during the Tudor period from Henry VIII's reign onwards. Remember that the native Irish tended to be Catholic. Label your living graph – from the viewpoint of the native Irish.

c Compare and contrast the two living graphs. What do these graphs show?

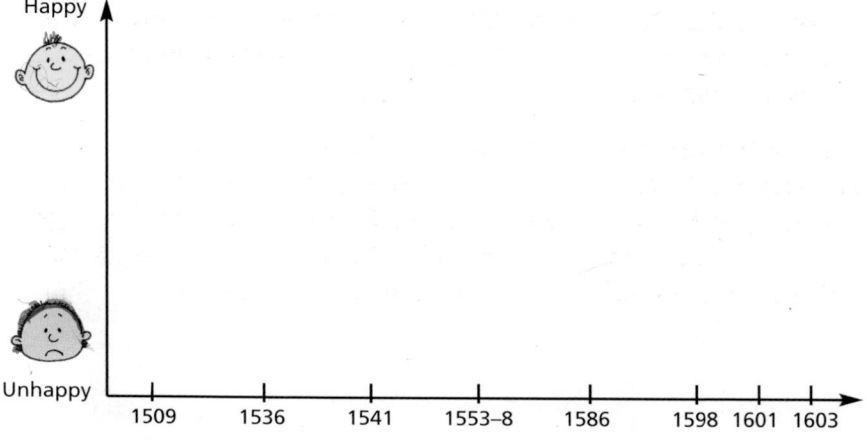

Happy / Unhappy graph with dates: 1509, 1536, 1541, 1553–8, 1586, 1598, 1601, 1603

HOW IS THE FLIGHT OF THE EARLS REMEMBERED TODAY?

In 2007, people commemorated an event known as the Flight of the Earls, which took place 400 years ago. In 1607 an Irish chieftain called Hugh O'Neill, Earl of Tyrone, and 100 followers left Lough Swilly and sailed from Ireland to Europe. Ireland was left without leaders and this enabled the English government to take lands in Ireland and give them to English and Scottish settlers. This was known as the Ulster plantation.

GET ACTIVE 3

See what you can find out about the Flight of the Earls using the internet and books from your school library or local library. You could present your information using the questions below.

Start with smaller questions, to consider the key details about the event:

- Who was involved?
- What happened?
- Why did it happen?
- When did it take place?
- Where did it take place?

Now think about some bigger questions, in order to consider the SIGNIFICANCE of the event:

- Why did the Flight of the Earls matter?
- What happened to land ownership after the Flight of the Earls?
- What were the effects of the Earls leaving Ireland?
- What other questions would you like to ask?
- How would you find the answers to these questions?

GET ACTIVE 4

The Flight of the Earls has been commemorated in different ways. Look at Sources 1–4 to see some of the ways an event in the past has been commemorated.

a What different aspects of the event have been remembered?

b Which source do you think commemorates the event in the best way? Why do you think that?

c What is the meaning of the words in Source 4?

SOURCE 1

Painting of the Flight of the Earls by Thomas Ryan painted in the 1960s.

SOURCE 2

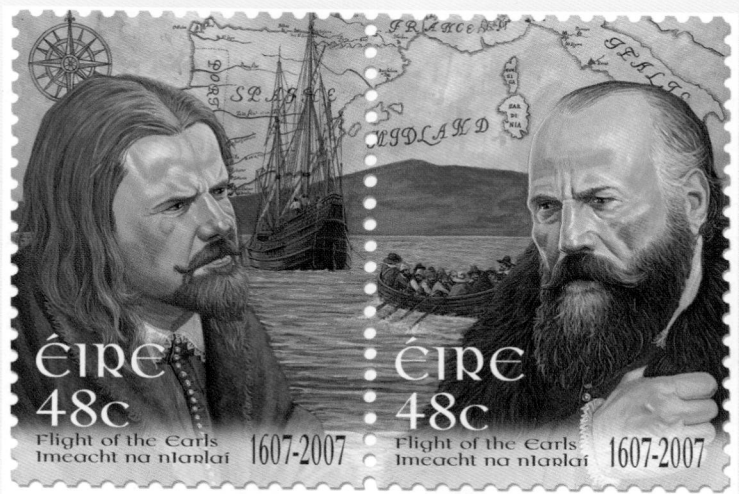

Two stamps commemorating the Flight of the Earls issued in February 2007.

SOURCE 3

This Christmas plate from 1972 features the 'Flight of the Earls'.

SOURCE 4

This song refers to when the Catholic leaders left Ireland in 1607. It makes a link with the 1980s when a lot of young people left Ireland to find work either in Britain or America. At the end of the song there is a hope that many would return to Ireland – which is happening today.

Extract from a song by Liam Reilly called 'Flight of Earls'

Flight of Earls
I can hear the bells of Dublin
in this lonely waiting room
And the paperboys are singin' in the rain
Not too long before they take us
to the airport and the noise
To get on board a transatlantic plane
We've got nothin' left to stay for,
We had no more left to say
And there isn't any work for us to do
So farewell ye boys and girls;
Another … Flight of Earls
Our best asset is our best export, too …

It's not murder, fear or famine
that makes us leave this time
We're not going to join McAlpine's Fusileers
We've got brains, and we've got visions; we've got
    education, too!
But we just can't throw away these precious years
So we walk the streets of London,
And the streets of Baltimore
We're the leaders of the future
But we're far away from home
And we dream of you beneath the Irish stars.

But if we see better days,
Those big airplanes go both ways
And we'll all be comin' back to you again!

GET ACTIVE 5

Using a circle time discussion, you could think about and discuss the following questions:

a Is there an event from the past that you celebrate? If so:

- Why is it important to you?
- How do you remember this event?
- Share your findings with a classmate and then with the rest of your class.

b What events are celebrated in your class? Make a class list.

c What events are commemorated in Northern Ireland, Ireland, Britain and Europe? Add to your class list.

d Why is it important to remember events from the past? Use examples from the list you have made.

e What might be the consequences for people if events are ignored or forgotten?

WHY DID MORE SETTLERS COME TO IRELAND IN THE EARLY 1600S?

You are going to investigate why it matters today that settlers came to Ireland during the Ulster plantation. Let's meet some of the people who were given land by the English crown after the Flight of the Earls.

Servitor

I am a soldier who fought for the English crown in Ireland during the Nine Years War 1594–1603. When the Treaty of Mellifont was signed in 1603, I saw there was an opportunity for the likes of us old soldiers to get a bit of land that was going. I couldn't believe my luck when the great O'Neill and his followers left Ireland in 1607.

I am delighted to be granted land, and I am even allowed to have Irish TENANTS, which I am glad about as I have a number of Irish friends now because of staying and living in Ireland. I must, however, promise to build a house and BAWN and keep arms just in case of attack. Servitors like me have been given a tenth of the plantation land.

London companies

I am a salter, which means I am a member of one of the guilds in the City of London. We were set up to help all those who traded in salt. Salt is very important to everyone as it preserves our food. My company and 55 other companies were 'invited' to finance the plantations of the County of Londonderry by the Crown.

In practice we were forced to carry out the plantation, even though many of our members did not wish to commit effort, money and lives to distant, barbarous, papist Ulster where things looked very dangerous. We were organised into twelve great companies, and had to raise money amongst ourselves to build the fortified city of Londonderry and the fortified town of Coleraine. In total the London companies were given a tenth of the plantation land.

English and Scottish settlers

We settlers have come to Ireland to gain land granted to us by the English crown. We are known as UNDERTAKERS, because we have undertaken to follow strict rules. For example, we are only allowed to have English or Scottish tenants on our land in Ireland and provide them with weapons.

We have to build a stone house with walls around it known as a house and bawn in order to protect ourselves. We pay the English crown a RENT and have to swear the OATH OF SUPREMACY, which means we have to be Protestant. We have also promised to introduce English methods of farming.

Life in Ireland is dangerous for us as some of the other settlers have been attacked by the Irish WOODKERNE. Undertakers like us have been given half of the plantation land (which was approximately 2,000,000 acres in total).

Loyal Irish

During the Nine Years War I remained loyal to the English crown. In return I was given land after 1607. I have the same rules to follow as the servitors. Unfortunately the land was only granted to me and not my children. So when I die the land will return to the English Crown.

The remaining plantation land was divided between loyal Irishmen like me, Trinity College, Dublin and a number of schools.

Church of Ireland

The Protestant Church of Ireland has been given one-fifth of the plantation land. Everybody has to pay TITHES (or a tenth of their income) to the Church of Ireland, even if they are Catholic or PRESBYTERIAN. This means that we as a church feel blessed by God because the land has given us a lot of money.

Native Irish woodkerne

I am a soldier who fought for the great Hugh O'Neill and the other Irish chieftains. When they left Ireland in 1607 my fellow soldiers and I were left leaderless and so took to the woods and mountains. When we saw these settlers come and take some of our best land we were angry, and so we tried to prevent the settlers from finishing their stone houses by attacking them. Having lost our lands we had very little money. We were reduced to stealing cattle and other goods from the settlers in order to survive.

GET ACTIVE 6

a Read carefully and extract the figures that show the land distribution during the plantation. Decide how you would like to represent that information. You could choose a pie chart or bar graph.

b What conclusion can you draw from your graph about which group got the most land?

c What do you learn from the viewpoint of the native Irish woodkerne?

HOW IS THE PLANTATION VIEWED TODAY?

SOURCE 5

These colonists brought to Ulster a way of life so very different from the rest of the country. Many had brought modern farming methods and a tradition of the PURITAN work ethic. In Ulster, as a result of Plantation, both landlord and tenant were usually Protestant and both spoke English.

The Race to Rule: Ireland and Europe 1570–1700 by A.M. Hodge written in 1998

SOURCE 6

A large number of settlers, mainly Scottish, took advantage of the opportunity to make a new beginning. In the main motivated by the Protestant faith, they had an assurance of forgiveness through faith in Christ Jesus and a new authority as each lived with conscience informed by the Bible. Each had a calling from God which translated into a new approach to work, not simply for loss or even for profit but for God.

Consequently barren land was cultivated into fertile farmland. Strong houses were built and improvements were made providing shelter from attack and better conditions for living. A sturdy people developed.

Politically the close relationship with the United Kingdom began; to everyone's benefit. Ulstermen played their part in the growth of the British EMPIRE, now the COMMONWEALTH. They had a sense of innovation and adventure as well as courage.

An extract from a pamphlet by Reverend Martin Smyth, an Ulster Unionist politician, 1986

A drawing of the plantation town of Coleraine, by Thomas Raven.

SOURCE 7

What did I have? said the fine Old Woman,
What did I have? this proud Old Woman did say,
I had four green fields – each one was a jewel,
But strangers came and tried to take them from me.
I had fine strong sons – they fought to save my jewels,
They fought and they died, and that was my grief, said she.

What have I now? said this fine Old Woman,
What have I now? this proud Old Woman did say,
I have four green fields, one of them's in bondage,
In strangers' hands, that tried to take it from me.
But my sons they have sons – as brave as were their fathers,
And my fourth green field will bloom once again, said she.

A song called 'Four Green Fields' by Tommy Makem

SOURCE 8

The sum of the plantation was the introduction of a foreign community which spoke differently, worshipped apart, and represented an alien culture and way of life. The more efficient methods of the new farmers, and the greater availability of capital which allowed the start of cottage industries, served to create further economic differences between Ulster and the rest of Ireland, and between Catholic and Protestant within Ulster. The deep resentment of the native Irish towards the Planters, and the distrustful siege mentality of the Planters towards the Irish, is a crude INTERPRETATION of the Irish problem today.

http://www.irelandseye.com/aarticles/history/events/conflict/bttc1.shtm

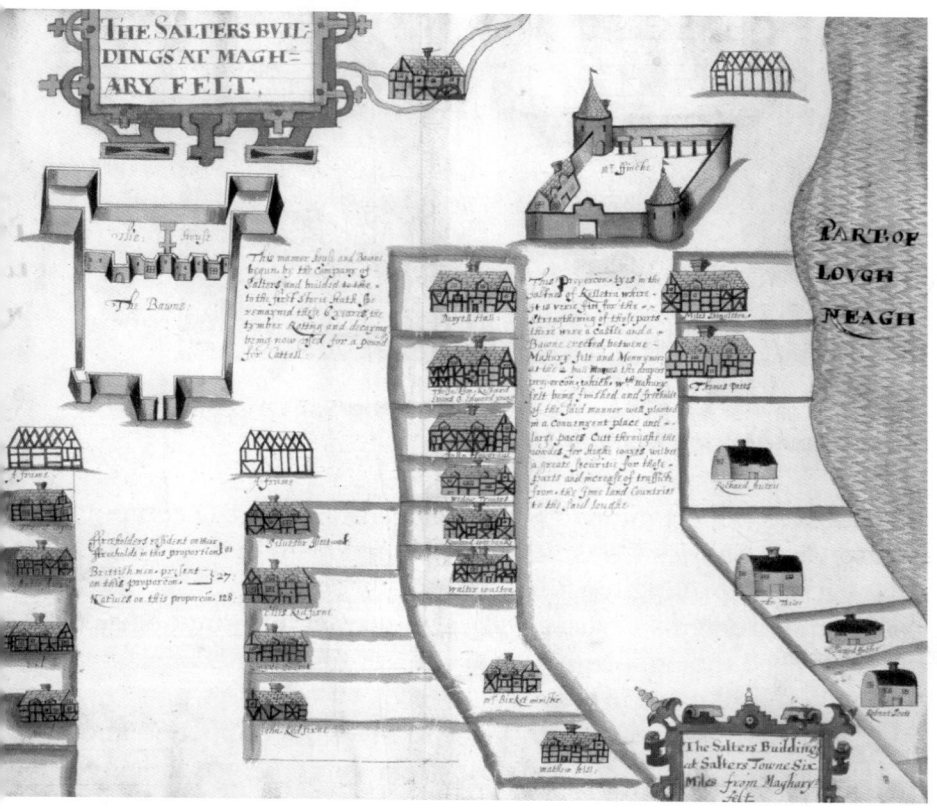

A map by Thomas Raven of the land of the Salters' Company.

GET ACTIVE 7

a Look carefully at Sources 5 and 6. Make a list of things that the Ulster plantation brought.

b Read Source 7. What do you think is the message of this song?

c In what ways does Source 7 differ from Sources 5 and 6?

d Can you give any reasons why these sources might differ?

e In what ways does Source 8 differ from Source 6?

f Using all the sources, make a list of the plus and minus points about the impact of the plantation on life today in Northern Ireland.

Having explored how and why settlers came to Ireland in the early 1600s, let's see how the plantation developed. We will look at some of the events that took place in Britain and Ireland at this time that affected the plantation and life today in Northern Ireland.

WHY DOES THE REBELLION IN 1641 MATTER TODAY?

GET ACTIVE 8

Look carefully at the banner on the right. You are going to make two lists.
a First write down what you can see in the banner.
b Then follow the enquiry below to see what happened in 1641, and then record what you think the message of the banner is today.

This is an ORANGE ORDER **Banner from the Rising Sons of Portadown Loyal Orange Lodge Number 273.**

In the 1640s important events took place in England, Scotland and Ireland. Charles I was having problems with his PARLIAMENT and ruling his kingdoms.

With the problems Charles was facing ruling his kingdoms, the Irish used the opportunity to try to get their lands back. A rebellion broke out in October 1641.

Let's look at some of the evidence to see what happened and to begin to understand why the rebellion matters even today.

GET ACTIVE 9

Using the internet, books in the school library and local library, try to find out what problems Charles I faced as king. You could use a mind map or your own visual diagram to record the information.

SOURCE 9

In October 1641, the Irish Catholics did rise all over Ireland at once: 200,000 persons were murdered.

R. Baxter, Autobiography *written in 1696*

SOURCE 10

Though the numbers were fantastically exaggerated (one Protestant historian put the Protestant dead at over 150,000, more than the entire population of Ireland at the time) on balance historians seem to think that about 12,000 Protestant men, women and children were either murdered or died of cold and starvation in 1641.

Robert Kee, Ireland, a History *written in 1980*

SOURCE 11

Driuinge Men Women & chi:dren by hund: reds vpon Briges & casting them into riuers, who drowned not were killed with poles & shot with muskets.

This is a picture from a set of playing cards sold in London after the rebellion. It is a Protestant's view of the killing of the Protestant settlers that took place on a bridge at Portadown in 1641.

Modern historians stress that the massacres of 1641 had a psychological impact on the Protestant settler community. Before the rebellion, relationships between the native Irish and the settlers had been improving. After it, many Protestants in Ireland took the attitude that the native Irish Catholic community could never be trusted again. This attitude led many settlers to take revenge on Catholics when they got the chance. In 1641–2, massacres of Catholic prisoners occurred at Kilwarlin woods near Newry, Rathlin Island, Glenmaquinn near Strabane and elsewhere. In 1642–3 a Scottish Covenanter army landed in Ulster. In addition, the English Parliament passed an Ordinance of 'No Quarter' against the Irish rebels, meaning that prisoners were to be killed when taken. William Lecky, the nineteenth-century historian of the rebellion, concluded that 'it is hard to know on which side the balance of cruelty rests'. The effects of the massacres of 1641 can still be seen in divisions in Northern Ireland today. Images of 1641 are still represented on the banners of the Orange Order.

SOURCE 12

The rebels increase daily in men and weapons. They use all kinds of cruelties in tormenting the poor Protestants, cutting off their private parts, ears, fingers and hands, plucking out their eyes, boiling the heads of little children before their mother's faces and then ripping up their mother's bowels. They kill the children as soon as they are born and rip up the mothers' bellies as soon as they have given birth. Men, women and children are driven to bridges and then cast down into the rivers. Those who do not drown are shot with muskets or have their brains pierced with poles. I pray to the Lord that England and Scotland will send relief to these afflicted Protestants.

This is an extract from a letter written by a man called Thomas Partington. He was in Ireland at the time of the rebellion and sent this letter to a friend in England at the end of November 1641.

GET ACTIVE 10

a How and why do Sources 9 and 10 differ?
b Read Source 12. What is the message of this source?
c In what ways does Source 11 support Source 12? Are these sources reliable?
d Now go back to Get Active 8 – what do you think the meaning of the Orange Order banner is today?

Ask yourself:

- Were the Protestant settlers the only people in the 1640s to suffer?
- How has history been used to justify a viewpoint today?
- Why is it important to look at other evidence about the past instead of just using one source?

SOURCE 13

IRISH EXAMINER

RESIDENTS PROTEST AS CROMWELL'S DEATH MASK IS DISPLAYED

22 May 2000

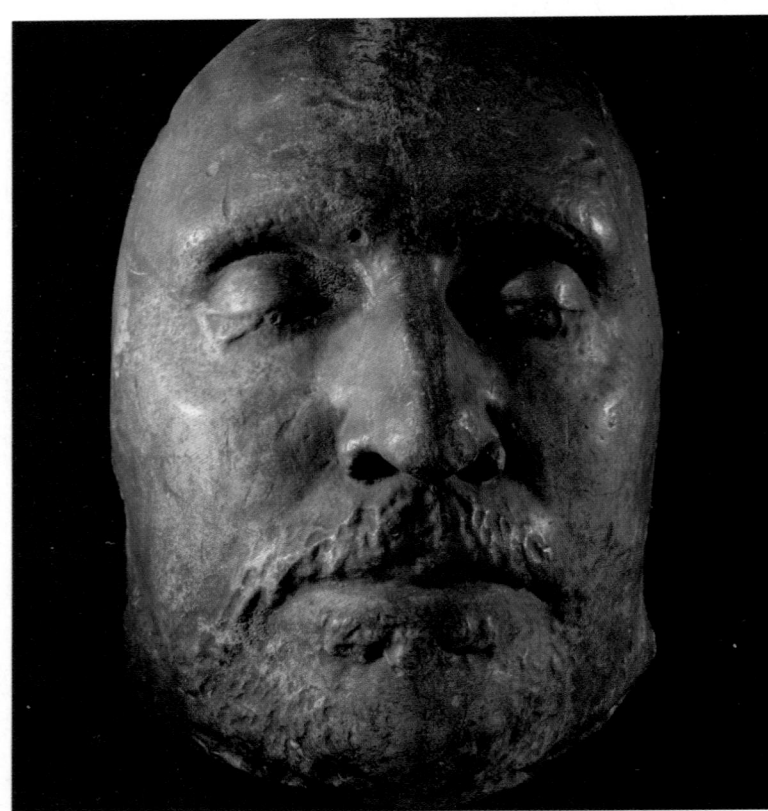

Demonstrators picketed a heritage centre yesterday as the death mask of Oliver Cromwell was put on display at the place where he was said to have massacred thousands of defenceless civilians.

The protest was staged at the Drogheda Heritage Centre after the cast of Cromwell's face, which was taken when he died from malaria in 1658, arrived on loan from the Cromwell Museum in Huntingdon, England.

The town's deputy mayor, Frank Godfrey, likened the exhibition to people showing off the head of Adolf Hitler to a Jewish community. 'The people in Drogheda suffered greatly. They were slaughtered, children, mothers and fathers,' he said. 'This man's face is the last thing we want to see. We don't forget and the people of Drogheda haven't forgotten.'

Cromwell landed in Ireland in August 1649 with an army of 12,000. His mission was to secure the new Commonwealth state he had just established in England from any royalist threat that might lurk in the Republic, and to rid the country of 'papal barbarism'. After overcoming Drogheda's defences of around 3,000 royalists, he is said to have ordered the slaughter of all the survivors.

But historian Tom Reilly, who organised the exhibition, said the criticisms of Cromwell are based on myth. 'His reputation was blackened by the spin-doctors of the English REFORMATION. He has been presented as a bloodthirsty dictator who killed thousands of innocent people, but there is no evidence to support this view,' he said. 'Those who died were soldiers who had been defending the town. Cromwell has to be seen in the context of a very violent time. He was scrupulous in his application of the rules of warfare as they then were. He was no worse than any other army leader in the 17th century,' Reilly said. 'By the standards of the day Cromwell was amazingly restrained and went to great lengths to ensure that his troops behaved in a disciplined way. He even hanged soldiers who were found stealing from locals and there is little to indicate that his orders to spare non-combatants at Drogheda were not followed.'

WHAT DO PEOPLE THINK ABOUT CROMWELL TODAY IN BELFAST?

SOURCE 14

A mural on Shankill Parade, West Belfast, 2002.

This is a mural painted in 2002 on Shankill Parade in Belfast.
The mural commemorates the life of Oliver Cromwell.
Cromwell is viewed as a hero for his role as defender of the
Protestant faith and his conquest of rebellious Catholic Ireland
in 1649–52. The mural shows four of Cromwell's New Model
Army (Roundheads) putting to death a native Irish rebel.

GET ACTIVE 11

You are going to look carefully at what
people think about Cromwell today.

a Look at Source 13. Make a list of facts in
this source. Make a list of opinions.

b Look at Source 14. What is fact? What is
opinion?

c Why did the people of Drogheda resent his
death mask coming to their town?

d What did you learn from the historian Tom
Reilly about Cromwell in Source 13?

e What viewpoint of Cromwell is given in the
mural in Belfast in Source 14?

f How has history been used in Sources 13
and 14 to justify a stereotypical viewpoint
of Cromwell? You could use these small
questions to help you discuss the big
question:

• Who has written/produced the source?
• Why has the source been
written/produced?
• Was the writer an eyewitness to the
events?
• How much fact or opinion is in the source?
• Has the author any reason to exaggerate
or distort the account?
• Is there other evidence to support this
source?

Plan, Do, Review

DOES THE ULSTER PLANTATION MATTER TODAY?

It is important to recognise that the past shapes life today, and events from the past have significance in people's lives today. In this chapter you have been thinking about why the plantation of Ulster matters today in Northern Ireland. You have also gained the opportunity to see how history can be used to create stereotypical viewpoints about the past.

You are going to produce a multimedia presentation to represent the significance of the Ulster plantation. Your presentation should show what can be done to check a source for bias, exaggeration or stereotyping.

PLAN

Stage 1

A multimedia presentation contains visuals and sounds. You could use ICT applications such as PowerPoint or Moviemaker. You could also use drama, song or mime to help you get your message across.

Get into groups and make a list of the tasks that need to be done in order to produce this presentation. You will have to work with others so think about the roles you need to assign to each other, for example, chairperson, designer, editor, presenter, etc.

Stage 2

Think about what you have learned about why the plantation matters today. You could use the grid below to help your group record their learning.

Event	What different viewpoints are there about these events today?	
1600s settlers from England and Scotland came to Ulster	Some Unionists view this event as the arrival of their forefathers who brought Protestantism, new ways of farming and wealth to Ulster. They set up towns and introduced Ulster Scots culture.	
1641 rebellion – the native Irish rebelled and attacked the settlers in order to regain their lands		
1649 Cromwell came to Ireland to end the rebellion begun in 1641		Some nationalists view this event as the end of Gaelic Ireland. Protestantism became the official religion and many Catholic Irish landowners lost their land.

DO

Create the multimedia presentation.

- What events are you going to show?
- How are you going to depict the events?
- What viewpoints are you going to show? Make sure your presentation shows different viewpoints.
- How are you going to show the need to challenge stereotypical viewpoints of the past?

REVIEW

Each group will assess the different multimedia presentations by the different groups. Your class can decide the CRITERIA by which the presentations will be assessed. An example is given for you in the table below:

Success Criteria	Poor 1	Satisfactory 2	Good 3	Very Good 4	Excellent 5
Content of the presentation – does it show why the plantation matters today and how to challenge stereotypical views of the past?					
Presentation – how well did the group use multimedia to make the presentation interesting?					

As a group, you could peer assess how well you think each person did their task in the group. Remember that when you are assessing someone else's work you need to be sensitive. The purpose of assessing each other's work is to help each other to improve. Try to give helpful tips of how things could improve.

Role	Rating (1 = poor, 5 = excellent)	Comment on how to improve
Chairperson		
Editor		
Designer(s)		
Presenter(s)		

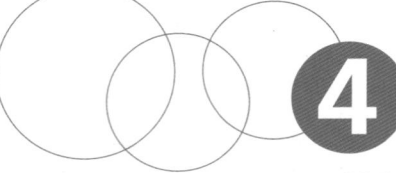

4 What did King William really think of Catholics?

 In this chapter we are learning to:
- ✓ understand what interpretations are;
- ✓ give reasons for different interpretations of William III;
- ✓ understand the origin of different interpretations;
- ✓ create your own interpretation of William III.

Who was King William?

I was born in The Hague in the Netherlands in 1650, and was quite a sickly little boy at first. I was a good scholar, and became a famous soldier in the Dutch army in 1668. I was King of England, Scotland and Ireland from 1689 until my death in 1702.

Meet the parents

My father was William II and he died ten days before my birth. He was Prince of Orange, which was a little state in south-west France.

My mother was Mary Stuart, an English princess and daughter of King Charles I (yes, the one who got beheaded). She never really liked living in the Dutch Republic and spent most of her time in France.

Meet the wife

I married Mary, the daughter of the Catholic king of England, James II, and we became joint rulers of England in 1689, when I was invited to take over the English throne by PARLIAMENT. This event was known as the Glorious Revolution. I accepted the English throne because I needed money and support to fight the war with France.

Meet my lifelong enemy

Louis XIV was King of France, one of the most powerful countries in Europe. I had to get other countries to unite with me against him in a Grand Alliance, as he was becoming too powerful. He had his eyes on parts of Italy, Germany and even my country, the Netherlands.

Painting of Louis XIV.

William of Orange Fact File

Born: 14 November 1650
Father: William II of Orange
Mother: Mary Henrietta Stuart, an English princess
Wife: Mary, daughter of James II, King of England
Children: None
Predecessor: James II
Interests: Fighting Louis XIV of France
Hobbies: Gardening, architecture and painting
Star sign: Scorpio
Buried: Kensington Palace
Death: Broke his collarbone by falling off his horse

Meet the father-in-law, James II

James II was in alliance with Louis XIV of France, because they were both Catholics, and this threatened the Dutch Republic. When I took the crown of England from James in 1689, he fled to Ireland for support among the Catholics, and I had to take an army over there to defeat him at the BATTLE OF THE BOYNE in 1690. I spent twelve weeks in Ireland before going off to Europe to fight Louis XIV.

James II, King of England, Scotland and Ireland from 1685 until December 1688.

GET ACTIVE 1

First impressions of William III

a Draw a timeline for William's life, from birth to death. Are there any events you find surprising, and can you give your reasons?

b Look at this website to find more information on William and to help you with the map question below: www.bbc.co.uk/northernireland/learning/william/

c Copy a blank map of Europe into your book, taking a full page. Write the title 'A Map of Europe at the time of William III, 1650–1702'. Mark on your map Orange/ The Dutch Republic/ France/ England/ Ireland. Beside each place match the following statements: Where I was born/ Where I was Stadholder in 1672 of the Dutch Republic/ Where Louis XIV was king / I was crowned king here in 1689/ I defeated James II here in 1690/ I settled Ireland and went off to Europe to finish my war against Louis.

d What do you notice about the length of time William spent in England and Ireland?

KING BILLY ON THE WALL

Among Northern Ireland unionists today William is known as King Billy, and his picture is celebrated on wall murals and Orange banners which you can see during the July celebrations.

Wall mural of King Billy, painted in Bangor, September 1997.

A painting of William III at the Battle of the Boyne 1690.

KING WILLIAM – A PROTESTANT, BUT DID THAT MEAN HE DID NOT LIKE CATHOLICS?

The wall mural was someone's recent idea, over 300 years after William died, of what he might have looked like. In history this is called an INTERPRETATION or someone's version of an event. But does it tell us what King William did, or what he thought about his Catholic subjects? Today William is seen as a Protestant king who was against the Pope and did not like Catholics.

In this chapter we will aim to uncover the real truth about William and the Catholics, and why interpretations like this survive about a man who spent 12 weeks of his life in Ireland.

KING WILLIAM HATED CATHOLICS – DO YOU AGREE OR DISAGREE?

Here are ten interpretations written by different historians about King William and the Catholics. Divide the class into two groups: the first group look at interpretations 1–5, the second group look at interpretations 6–10, and then share ideas.

1. One of the reasons William gave for taking the throne of England was to free England from the rule of the Catholic James II.

2. William passed anti-Catholic laws, called the PENAL LAWS, in Ireland in 1691 after the Battle of the Boyne. These laws prevented Catholics from practising their religion and from having a say in who ran the country.

3. William had a very anti-Catholic reputation. He spent most of his adult life fighting wars against Catholic rulers like James II of England and Louis XIV of France.

4. When he landed at Brixham in England in 1683, William said: 'The Liberties of England and the Protestant religion I will defend.' William was soon the champion of the Protestant religion against the supposed evils of Popery and the Catholic religion.

5. 'No Catholic shall inherit the throne of England.' William supported the passing of the Act of Settlement in 1701 that excluded Catholics from ever becoming monarch of England.

6. A Catholic hymn of praise, called a Te Deum, was reputedly sung for William in St Patrick's Cathedral, Dublin, in 1690 as part of a thanksgiving service for his arrival.

7. One of William's allies against France was Italy, a Catholic country ruled by the Pope, who supported William in his attempt to keep France from becoming too powerful.

8. William was not anti-Catholic, even though he was a committed Protestant. He needed money from the English parliament as he was constantly at war, so he had to support them in their bid to eliminate Catholics' influence in their government.

9. In 1691, the year after his victory over King James at the Boyne, William allowed the Irish Parliament to pass the Penal Laws against Catholics. But he didn't stay in Ireland to enforce them, and hurried off to Europe to continue his war against France.

10. William treated the defeated Catholic supporters of James II with respect, and ordered no punishment for them. He hanged a soldier when he heard that he had killed JACOBITE prisoners, and in Waterford he oversaw the safe exit of the defeated garrison, and left instructions that the Catholic inhabitants were not to be treated cruelly.

GET ACTIVE 4

a Read the five interpretations you have been allocated, and discuss whether you agree or disagree with the statements.

b Get into pairs and copy the 'Interpretation Line' below onto a large sheet of paper.

William hated Catholics

AGREE ——————————————— DISAGREE

c Write down at least two reasons why you have reached your conclusion and share your points with the rest of your group.

d Listen to the feedback from the other group. Can you suggest reasons why there would be these differences?

e Look at the cartoon on the right showing why historians would say different things about William. How do their ideas compare with yours?

43

WHY DO HISTORIANS DISAGREE ABOUT WILLIAM?

You have discovered that different interpretations of William exist; and you have looked at some of the reasons why historians' views about him differ. Now we will look at some more evidence to try to uncover the truth.

What exactly do historians argue about?

When historians argue, or have different views about interpretations in history, it is called a controversy. Historians often have great debates or arguments over interpretations of William's rule. But what is it that is so controversial about William, and causes so many discussions and arguments among historians, even today?

Was William really the Pope's enemy?

Painting of King William's arrival in Ireland in 1689.

If you have ever visited the Grand Opera House in Belfast, you will see a copy of this painting illustrated on the doors of the theatre. It is supposed to be the work of Pieter Van de Meulen, who worked at William's court in the seventeenth century. It shows William's arrival in Ireland as part of his campaign to defeat James II. In 2006, the BBC journalist Mark Devenport wrote an article which said that when the painting was first put on show in STORMONT buildings in the 1930s, it caused such a stir that it had to eventually be removed to a less prominent position. Visit the website http://news.bbc.co.uk/1/hi/northern_ireland/5263210.stm to read Mark Devenport's full story.

Let's look at the facts of the story. In 1933, some Unionists in the Stormont government bought the painting and agreed to display it in a prominent place where a lot of people could see it. They thought it would show William on his way to the Boyne to victory over the Catholic King James.

Can you imagine their surprise when they first saw the painting, because there above William's head was someone who looked like the Pope giving William his blessing! To some Unionists living in the 1930s, this painting did not fit in with their ideas about William and the Pope. The painting was vandalised in 1933 by two visiting Glasgow councillors, one of whom threw red paint over it, while the other slashed the figure of the Pope. In 1975 it was given to the Public Records Office in Belfast, but today it is kept in the Speakers Office in Stormont.

The figure supposed to be Pope Innocent XI.

GET ACTIVE 5

a Look at the painting. Can you see any evidence to suggest that William did not like Catholics? Is there any evidence to prove that William was against the Pope? What do you already know to be a fact about William and the Pope?

b Can you think of any reasons why this painting would have upset some Unionists in the 1930s? Do you think anyone would still be offended by the message of the painting today?

WAS WILLIAM REALLY A PROTESTANT SAVIOUR AND CHAMPION?

SOURCE 1 William in, James out

Dublin's Protestants began to take revenge against Catholics just hours after King James fled Ireland for France following his defeat at the Battle of the Boyne. On 3 July word was sent to King William to come and restore order. The news that he was on his way was greeted with joy. Dublin's Protestants were terrified that the Jacobite forces might return. If Derry had been besieged, might Dublin be next? Their greatest fear was of a rerun of the 1641 rebellion, which led to the massacre of hundreds of Protestants.

From BBC historian and producer Patrick Speight on his website about King Billy in 2002

SOURCE 2

During the period of the Penal Laws in Ireland, the ruling class became Protestant. They were the only people who could sit in parliament, but they were only 10 per cent of the 5 million population in Ireland at that time. They also controlled 95 per cent of the land.

Modern history textbook: The Protestant Ascendancy

SOURCE 3

William allowed some of his supporters to make anti-Catholic speeches in the year before the Glorious Revolution, not for religious reasons but for political ones, to help him get the support of Protestants in the English parliament. In fact William was a very tolerant man who respected all religions.

A modern historian, J. Gibney

GET ACTIVE 6

a Read the three sources above and then match the number of each statement below to the number of the source. This source tells me that:
   i)   William was more interested in the war in Europe than defending the Protestant religion.
   ii) After William's reign the most important people in politics and government in Ireland were Protestant.
   iii) Some Protestants in Ireland looked to William to save them from the threat of another Catholic rebellion, and to make them feel that their land and property would be secure.

b What do you think William really thought about Catholics?

c Why would historians and others say this about him?

HOW CAN WE EXPLAIN THE DIFFERENT INTERPRETATIONS OF WILLIAM III?

There are many interpretations of William III, and if we are to understand them fully we must look at the reasons why they were created in the first place, and also how they were created.

SOURCE 4

The recent book and TV series called *Battlefield Britain*, produced by Peter and Dan Snow, showed the Battle of the Boyne as one of the great battles in British history. Search the internet to see more details about the book.

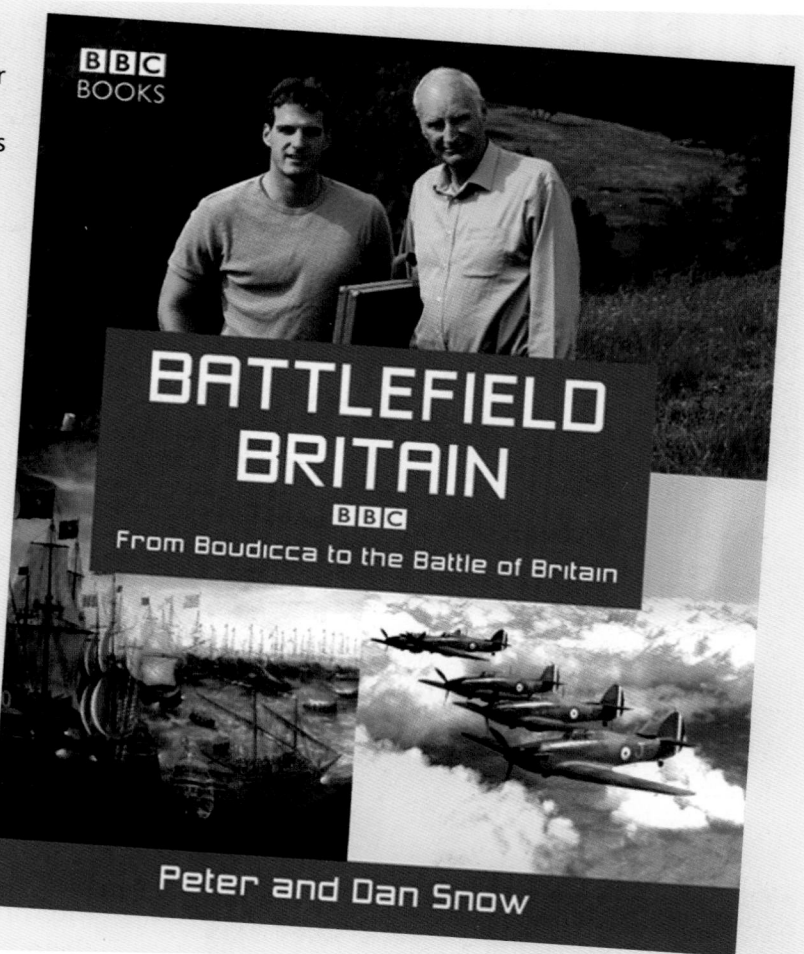

SOURCE 5

An anti-Catholic song called 'Lillibulero' was written before the Battle of the Boyne and sung by anti-Jacobite supporters in Ireland. In the song James II's right-hand man Tyrconnell is criticised for giving top government jobs to Catholics.

> Now Tyrconnell is come ashore
>
> And we shall have commissions galore.
>
> And everyone that won't go to Mass
>
> He will be turned out to look like an ass.

This is just an extract – the whole song can be found on the internet

SOURCE 6

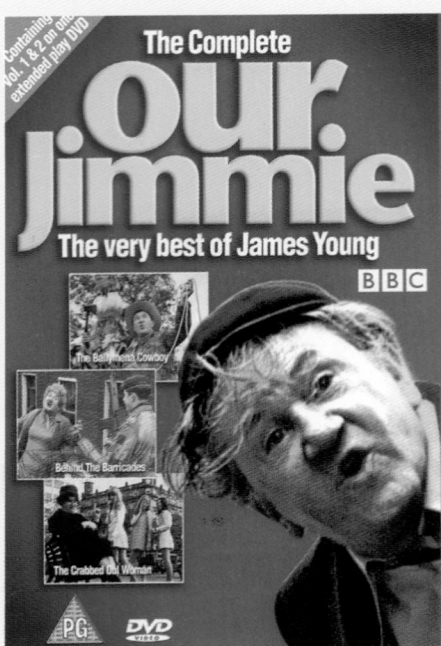

This is a DVD compilation of the sketches of James Young, an Ulster comedian who performed on stage and TV in the 1950s. In his William of Orange sketch, he dresses up as King William. (Visit the BBC website to get the full sketch.)

SOURCE 7

Bronze statue of William III in Dublin.

GET ACTIVE 7

a Put each of the four sources into one of the following categories of interpretation:
  - Film, TV programme or documentary
  - Building or physical remain
  - Book
  - Poem or song
  - Painting or sculpture

b Look at the list of reasons why interpretations in history are made (below). Match each statement to one of the sources (4–7):
  - To make people laugh.
  - To entertain people.
  - To inform people.
  - To give accurate information.
  - To attract visitors or crowds.
  - To make money.
  - To commemorate something.

c What does each of the interpretations tell you about why the artist made it?

d Does it matter if the interpretation provides accurate information?

Plan, Do, Review

In this chapter you have looked at the reasons why interpretations like the one we have examined in detail may exist, and also why historians would have different interpretations of William. Your task is now to choose your own interpretation of William III for the cover of a programme advertising an exhibition called 'William – a Protestant hero and champion'.

PLAN

Read carefully over your work in this chapter and begin to look at the different ways that William has been portrayed. Visit the website: http://www.bbc.co.uk/northernireland/ learning/william/orange.shtml and find images or examples of each of the following interpretations, and explain your choices.

- Paintings or murals showing examples of William as a Protestant hero.
- Statue or building connected with William and the Protestant religion.
- Examples of anti-Catholic PROPAGANDA, e.g. books, pamphlets or posters.
- Anti-Catholic laws passed in William's reign.
- Anti-Catholic songs, poems or music connected with William.
- Anti-Catholic written interpretations of William by historians.

DO

Now choose the **one** image, picture or information that you will use on your front cover. Explain to a partner why and how you made your selection.

REVIEW

Listen to the choices other people in your class made. Make a note of three different interpretations you liked, and say which one you most agree with and why.

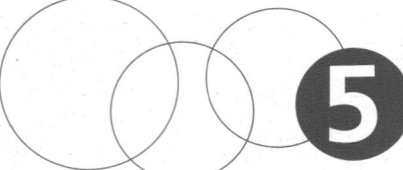

5 The Revolution Bug – how and why did it spread?

In this chapter we are learning to:
- ✓ identify the causes and consequences of revolutions;
- ✓ make links between cause and effect;
- ✓ be creative in designing a visual representation of your learning.

Have you heard of the word revolution? What does it mean? It comes from the word *revolve* which means to turn around. Think of a bicycle wheel turning around. When a revolution happens in a country it means that things get turned around. How the country is ruled, and how people are organised in society, changes. In this chapter you are going to investigate some revolutions that took place in the eighteenth century, to find out how and why Ireland caught the revolution bug.

GET ACTIVE 1

a How would you try to change something today, for example in your local area or in your school? Some examples are suggested below. Can you think of any others?

writing a letter   a protest march   using your school council

talking to a teacher or community representative   violence   petition

using local radio   fundraising

b Discuss which methods would be most successful, and why.
c Discuss which approaches would be least successful, and why.

We are going to think about what causes a revolution, and consider whether revolutions are always the best way to change things. You will investigate the methods people use during a revolution, and then consider the consequences of revolutions, to see whether things change for the better. We are going to look at three revolutions in this chapter.

The American Revolution 1775–83. This is a painting of Washington crossing the River Delaware.

The French Revolution 1789. This is a painting of the Tennis Court Oath, 20 June 1789.

The failed revolution of the United Irishmen's Rebellion 1798. This is a painting of the Battle of Ballynahinch, 1798.

GET ACTIVE 2

Look carefully at the three paintings of the revolutions.

a How have the artists chosen to show these events from the past? Make a list of different words to describe the three different paintings.

b In what ways have the artists shown the events in a positive light? Can you explain why this may be so?

c Do you think these are accurate pictures of what really happened in the past? Explain your answer.

LET'S LOOK AT THE AMERICAN REVOLUTION (1775–83)

Remember that in Chapter 2 you learned that the first COLONY set up by England was in Jamestown in America in 1607. By the 1700s, thirteen colonies had been established in North America. They flourished and had become rich.

Between 1775 and 1783 the Americans decided to end the rule of the thirteen colonies in America by fighting the American War of INDEPENDENCE against Britain. This has become known as the American Revolution. Let's find out what happened. The story is told on pages 53–55.

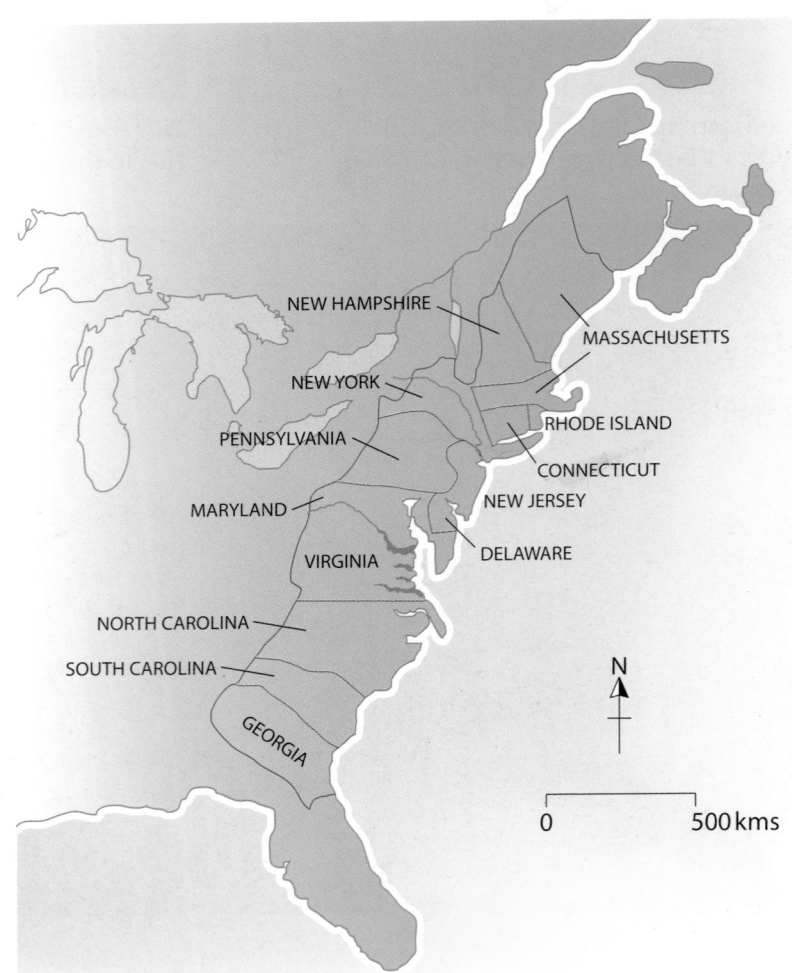

Map of the thirteen colonies. At the outbreak of the revolution, America was only a strip of land on the east of the continent.

GET ACTIVE 3

a Look closely at the story of the American Revolution in the four boxes on page 53, and list the reasons you can find to explain why the Americans were unhappy.

b As you read about the events, try to extract the key events and make your own timeline.

c Discuss your timeline with a partner. What are you learning about what causes revolutions?

1770–5

"Taxation without representation is tyranny."

James Otis.

A war called the Seven Years War (1756–63) between Britain, Prussia and Hanover against France, Austria, Russia, Sweden and Spain had cost Britain a lot of money. Britain decided that the colonies in America should help to pay the huge debt. After all, Britain had protected them during the Seven Years War. Britain introduced a series of TAXES that the American colonists hated. The colonists used the slogan that the PARLIAMENTARIANS during the English civil war had used, 'No taxation without representation'. James Otis, a lawyer from Massachusetts, made the phrase 'Taxation without representation is TYRANNY' famous.

In March 1770, the colonists held a protest in Boston. British soldiers opened fire on a crowd of protesters and killed five people. This was known as the Boston Massacre, and the event brought great support for those in America who were calling for independennce from Britain.

Paul Revere's famous engraving of the Boston Massacre published in the *Boston Gazette* 12 March 1770.

THE DESTRUCTION OF TEA AT BOSTON HARBOR.

The Boston Tea Party.

Boston continued to be a centre of opposition to the British government. In 1773, Britain tried to sell lots of cheap tea to the colonies in America, which British merchants had bought from India. This made the colonists angry, as the cheap tea would mean they would have to lower the price of the tea they had produced and so lose money. In December 1773 a group of Boston men dressed up as Indians and boarded the British ships carrying the cheap tea. They threw the tea into Boston harbour. This has become known as the Boston Tea Party. The British PARLIAMENT closed the port of Boston and this angered many Americans as they believed that Britain wanted to take away their right to govern themselves.

In September 1774 representatives of twelve colonies met in Philadelphia to form the First Continental Congress. The thirteenth colony, Georgia, soon joined them. The colonies condemned the harsh treatment of the British parliament, voted to stop IMPORTING British goods, and called on all Americans to begin gathering soldiers. The colonies were acting together to defend their rights. The British government was angry and agreed to use force if necessary to restore order in the American colonies. The REVOLUTIONARY war was about to begin.

Peyton Randolph, the President of the First Continental Congress.

1775–89

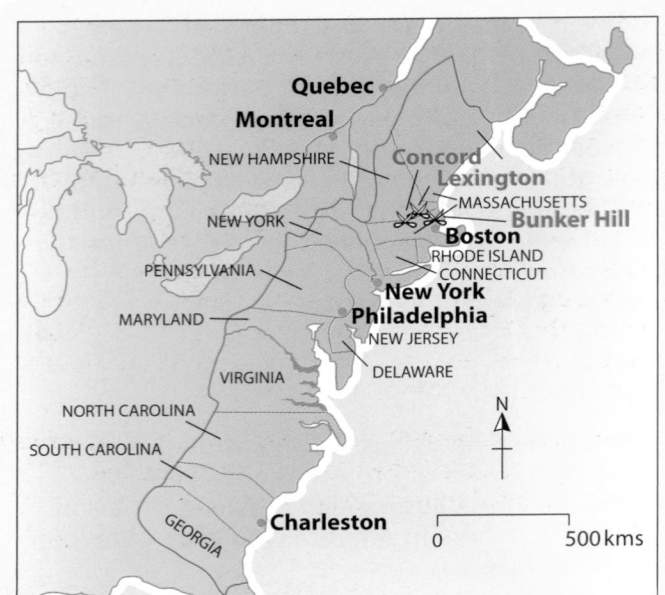

The first fighting of the REVOLUTIONARY war took place at Lexington in April 1775 when the British sent a regiment to CONFISCATE arms and arrest revolutionaries in Concord. The revolutionaries refused to give up their arms and instead made a stand at Lexington near Boston. The British came under heavy fire and were forced to retreat to Boston. Other colonies sent troops to join the revolutionaries and a battle was fought between the American revolutionaries and the British at Bunker Hill in June 1775. The British won but had a lot of casualties, and in March 1776 they decided to evacuate Boston.

Map of events during the American revolution.

On 4 July 1776, the Second Continental Congress decided that only independence from Britain would solve the Americans' problems with Britain. They signed the United States Declaration of Independence. This contained a long list of things the Americans thought the Westminster parliament had done wrong.

Thomas Jefferson presents the Declaration of Independence to the Second Continental Congress. Benjamin Franklin is on his left and John Hancock, President of the Congress, is seated behind the table.

The British army returned in force and took New York, then in 1777 captured Philadelphia. The British, however, were defeated at Saratoga in October 1777 (as depicted in the painting). This event showed that the Americans could beat the British, and it encouraged Britain's old enemy France to enter the war on America's side in 1778. In 1779 Spain and the Dutch became allies of the Americans, leaving Britain to fight the war alone. These allies helped the Americans with money and troops to fight the British.

The surrender of the British at Saratoga on 17 October 1777. This was a major morale boost for the Americans and encouraged France to enter the war on the American's side.

After the British were defeated at Yorktown in October 1781, they became war-weary. Although the British fought further battles, eventually they were defeated and signed a peace treaty in 1783. The US CONSTITUTION was agreed in 1788 and George Washington became the first president in 1789. Washington had been a commander of the American army during the War of Independence, and this made him a natural candidate for the new position of President. America had overthrown the rule of the British monarchy, set up a republic and brought greater freedoms for the people of the new United States. Who would be next to catch the revolutionary bug? The French monarchy had spent a lot of money helping the Americans, and those French who fought in America returned to France with new ideas about how a country could be ruled without a monarch.

George Washington had been a commander of the American army during the War of Independence. This made him a natural candidate for the new position of President.

GET ACTIVE 4

Look at the revolution bicycle below. On one wheel it has headings which show the main causes of the revolution; on the other it has headings which show the main effects.

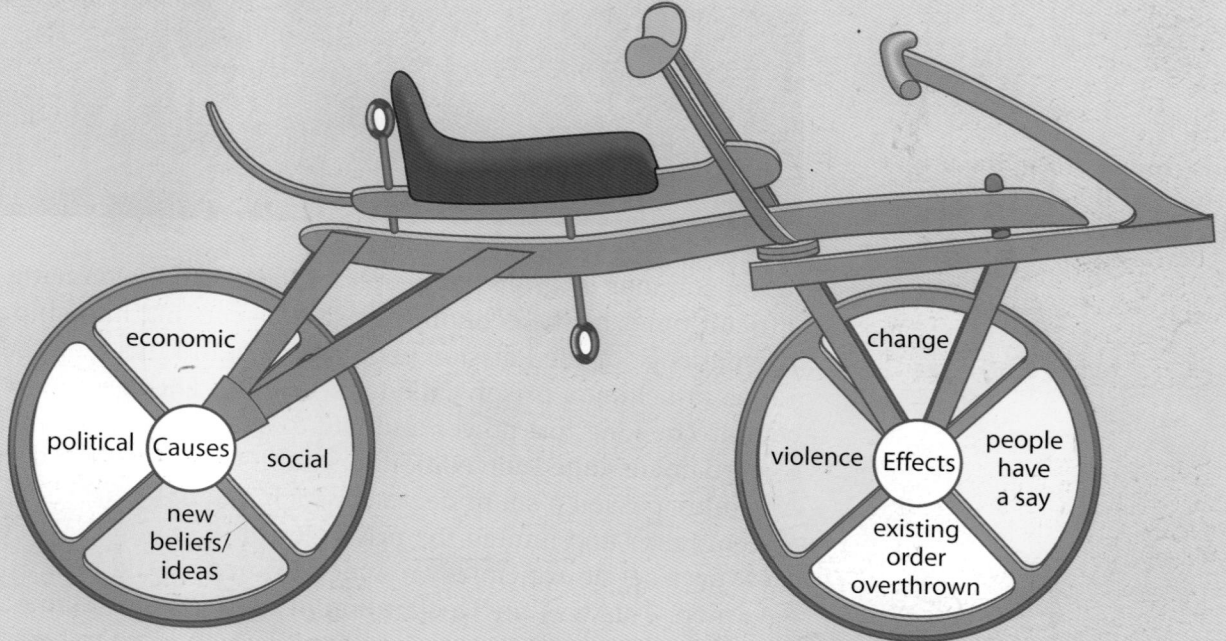

a Make a copy of the revolution bicycle.

b Alongside each of the causes, write in examples from the information on pages 52–5.

c Alongside each of the effects, write in examples along the spokes.

d Draw an individual on the bicycle, and list the names of the important individuals of the American Revolution. You may have to do some more research to find as many individuals as possible.

WHY DID THE FRENCH CATCH THE REVOLUTIONARY BUG IN 1789?

In the 1780s France was in crisis. The population had increased and food shortages were made worse by bad harvests in 1787–9. Food prices were high and the people had to pay high taxes. The poor were becoming desperate. In contrast, the French king and queen lived in great luxury. They were running up huge bills, and there was not enough money to pay for this luxury. Many people in France felt that this was unfair, and something should be done to make sure that people were treated fairly. The king made all the decisions in France.

Paris crowds storm the prison fortress of the Bastille on 14 July 1789.

In the summer of 1789, the people of Paris had been facing difficult times as the economic crisis was causing hardship. The patience of the Parisian people broke, and this resulted in a mob attacking a prison called the Bastille. The revolution had begun. The king lost power and had to share power with a kind of parliament called the National Assembly. The National Assembly passed a set of decrees which made the taxation system fairer and limited the privileges of the nobility. They drew up a set of principles on which France should be governed. This was the Declaration of the Rights of Man, which abolished slavery; decreed that women were to be treated equally; and set up a legislative assembly to pass the laws in France instead of the king making all the decisions. The king refused to support the decrees or the Declaration, which led the Assembly to question the role of the king.

In April 1792 France went to war against Austria and Prussia. The war was costly for France. The war went badly and the French people looked for someone to blame. In early September 1792 mobs attacked the prisons and killed people they thought were undermining France in the war. On 20 September 1792 the National Assembly abolished the monarchy and declared France to be a republic. Louis XVI was no longer king. Many people believed that Louis should be punished for his tyranny. Some even believed that he was undermining France by giving secrets to the Austrians – because his wife Marie Antoinette was Austrian. Louis was put on trial and found guilty. He was executed on 21 January 1793 and his wife Marie Antoinette was executed in October 1793.

The public execution of Louis XVI, 21 January 1793.

The revolution went wrong and a terror broke out. All the faults in the country largely caused by the war were blamed on CONSPIRATORS. These so-called 'conspirators' included the rich and anybody who criticised the revolution. For many people life was no better under the revolution than under the monarchy. In 1804 Napoleon Bonaparte became emperor. For many people, life was still as hard during the revolution as it was during the monarchy.

WHAT WERE THE REASONS FOR THE FRENCH REVOLUTION?

Life for me is very difficult. The harvests were bad last year and so food prices are very high. I have six children and have to feed them. There are so many families in France looking for land. With an increase in the mouths to feed and less land to farm, life is impossible. We only have a small piece of land, one chicken and a cow. Yet we have to pay 20 kg of wheat and three chickens every year to one noble and 60 kg of oats and one chicken to another noble person. On top of all this we also have to pay TITHES to the church. Something needs to be done to make life easier. Why should we suffer when the rich live so well?

I am a craftsman selling wooden furniture. The king is placing a lot of taxes on people. This means with the high food prices and high taxes, fewer people want to buy furniture. I am running out of money and my family is beginning to go hungry. I saw pictures on the streets of Paris yesterday showing the king and queen living in great splendour. This is unfair and the king must do something to help us or else he must go. It would be better if the people had more say, then there would be less corruption and more money to go round fairly.

I am a businessman and I am angry at the king for the way that France is being ruled. The king and queen are corrupt, and why should we work so hard for the likes of them to live off us by charging such high taxes? Every year the taxes increase, and this is due to the king and queen wasting money. The MIDDLE CLASSES are the ones making France great through our businesses. We need to have more say in how the country is run. We would make better decisions than the king. I have been reading a great book by Rousseau, who says that everybody is born equal, so why then do we live with inequality in France? We should do the same as the Americans did, overthrow the rulers who were oppressing them!

I always thought Louis should not have married an Austrian. They are our enemies and now Marie Antoinette's extravagance is bleeding France dry. The king is trying to tax us, and there are rumours that we will lose our feudal dues. How dare he insult me as a nobleman to ask for taxes when he cannot control his spending? If the king does not rule us better, all of France will be in chaos. This will be dangerous for me. Louis must not let the riffraff have a say in how France is ruled, or else we will all be ruined.

As king of France I want to make the country great. I had to fight wars, which have left the country with debt, in order to protect France. I have to ask for taxes so that France can have a good navy and enough soldiers just in case countries like Britain or Austria attack us. I believe God has appointed me as king and no one has the right to remove me. I believe that it is my role to serve the people of France.

GET ACTIVE 5

a Look carefully at the opinions of the five people in France. There are many different reasons for the revolution in France. List the reasons that the people give for why France had a revolution.

b Now try to sort the information into the four categories given in the spokes of the wheel below: political, economic, social and ideas.

c Which reasons do you think were short term?

d Which reasons do you think were long term?

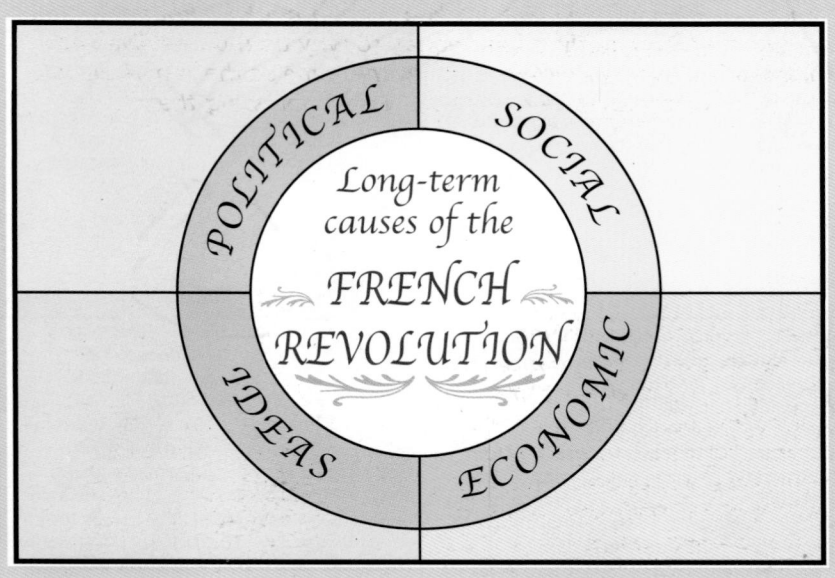

GET ACTIVE 6

a What good things did the revolution bring for the people of France?

b What bad things did the revolution bring for the people of France?

c Overall, do you think the revolution was good for France? Explain your answer.

UNITED IRISHMEN'S REBELLION 1798 – HOW AND WHY DID THE REVOLUTION BUG SPREAD TO IRELAND?

America

There were close links between America and Ireland. In 1771, Benjamin Franklin visited Ireland and suggested co-operation between his PATRIOTS in Ireland and the American colonists in their struggle against the British. Approximately half of the American colonials in 1776 were of Irish ancestry. It is estimated that 240,000 Protestants had emigrated from the north of Ireland to America and 100,000 Catholics from the rest of Ireland. Many in Ireland looked to America as an example of how to gain independence and break the British control of Ireland.

France

People in Ireland looked to France to see examples of change in how the country was ruled. For example, people were granted religious freedom, which meant they could go to the church of their choice. There was a new system of voting that allowed ordinary people to vote, and a new form of government called a Republic was created. These changes appealed to PRESBYTERIANS and Catholics in Ireland who were excluded from voting as a result of the PENAL LAWS.

> ### GET ACTIVE 7
>
> a In what ways did the events in America influence Ireland?
> b In what ways did the events in France affect Ireland?

Why were some Irish people unhappy in the 1790s?

> ### GET ACTIVE 8
>
> a Place the reasons for why people were unhappy in rank order.
> b You could record your information on a pyramid diagram.

Catholics, Presbyterians and QUAKERS were unhappy because they could not vote as a result of the Penal Laws. They had to pay a tax called a tithe to the Church of Ireland, even though they had their own churches to attend.

People in Ireland were unhappy that most laws for Ireland were made in London. They felt that the Irish parliament did not have enough say. They wanted Irish people making laws for Ireland instead of English people having all the say in how it was governed.

RELIGIOUS REASONS / POLITICAL REASONS / ECONOMIC REASONS / SOCIAL REASONS

The population of Ireland in the 1750s was approximately 2.5 million. By 1790 the population had doubled to 5 million. With this increase in population, land became scarce. Rent for land and tithes were increasing but wages were falling. Britain's war with France, begun in 1792, had increased taxes in Ireland. Poor people were finding life very difficult.

Many people were reading about new ideas of the ENLIGHTENMENT. This included new ideas about:
• how to structure society, i.e. avoiding one ruler deciding everything
• giving more equality to people, i.e. taking away privileges from the rich to help the poor
• allowing more people to have a say in making decisions about how the country was governed.
These new ideas raised hopes for people that things could be better.

WHY DID THE UNITED IRISHMEN'S REBELLION BREAK OUT?

Some people in Ireland decided to use the examples of America and France to begin their own revolution to try to make things better for all the people of Ireland. These people were known as the United Irishmen. Let's find out what happened to them, and what happened to their revolution.

1779–98

In October 1779, the Irish parliament got its own say by being able to pass a law which allowed FREE TRADE between Ireland and Britain. Before this law was passed, there was a charge on Irish goods going to Britain which made Irish goods expensive in Britain. Free trade was better for the Irish as it meant that people in Britain would be happier to buy Irish goods.

The experience of free trade showed people in Ireland the benefits of the Irish parliament having a greater say in how things in Ireland were run. In 1782 the Irish parliament passed a constitution. This promised Ireland its own parliament and legal system.

Henry Grattan addressing the Irish parliament.

Theobald Wolfe Tone, a Protestant, founded the Society of United Irishmen in Belfast. It was a group of both Protestants and Catholics. They hoped to bring together Irishmen of all backgrounds in order to achieve religious equality and to reform the way Ireland was governed. They took many ideas from the French revolution, believing that the only way to change things was to overthrow the old corrupt system by any means necessary.

Theobald Wolfe Tone.

When war broke out between Britain and France in 1792, the British government saw the United Irishmen as a threat. They placed strict controls on the Society, for example, all public meetings were banned and there was a ban on the distribution of unlicensed weapons. In 1796, the British government introduced the death penalty for anybody who took an oath of loyalty which was against the law. The picture here shows the United Irishmen taking an oath against English rule. Anyone who took this oath would now face the death penalty.

Members of the Society of United Irishmen taking an oath against English rule.

Wolfe Tone left Ireland for America in 1795 because of the strict controls. In 1796 he went to France to get support to launch a rebellion in Ireland. Bad weather prevented the French force of 43 ships and 15,000 men from landing in Bantry Bay in Ireland. Tone went back to France. Meanwhile the British government placed even stricter controls on Ireland. They used spies to find out about the plans of the United Irishmen's rebellion. MARTIAL LAW was declared in Ireland in March 1798.

1798

The United Irishmen's rebellion was planned for 23 May 1798, but the government found out about the plans from their spies. The key leaders were arrested on 19 May. One leader, Lord Edward Fitzgerald, was mortally wounded.

The arrest of Lord Edward Fitzgerald.

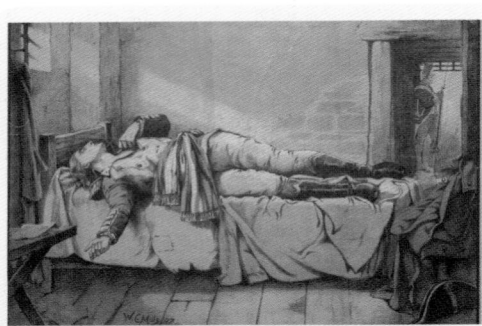

The arrest of the leaders weakened the rising in Dublin, but the rebellion took place in Wexford, Carlow, Kildare and Meath. The rebels were poorly armed and organised. They were outnumbered by the government forces. The rebels were defeated at the Battle of Vinegar Hill on 21 June 1798. Risings broke out in early June in Antrim and Down, under the leadership of Henry Joy McCracken and Henry Munro. The United Irishmen were defeated in Ulster, and Munro and McCracken were hanged.

The Battle of Vinegar Hill.

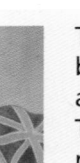

A French fleet tried to land in Donegal in October 1798. Six French ships and their crews were captured. Wolfe Tone was among those French officers captured, and was court martialled (put on trial by military law) and sentenced to death. He took his own life. The revolution had failed, and the event was remembered in history as the United Irishmen's rebellion.

Wolfe Tone taking his own life.

GET ACTIVE 9

Make your own flowchart of the events of the United Irishmen's rebellion.

GET ACTIVE 10

a How are decisions made today in Northern Ireland? Try to make a list of all the different people in our society who can make decisions that affect us.

b Who can vote? You could search the internet to find out who can vote and how people vote.

c What did the United Irishmen hope to achieve?
  - In what ways have the aims of the United Irishmen been achieved today?
  - In what ways have they not been achieved?

WHY DID THE REVOLUTION BUG NOT SUCCEED IN IRELAND?

There are a number of reasons to explain the failure of the United Irishmen's rebellion:

1 The government used very harsh forms of torture to find out about anybody planning to undermine it, especially during a time of war with France.
2 Spies and informers were used by the government to find out the plans of the rising. This led to the arrest of the leaders and weakened the rising right from the start.
3 There was a lack of communication between the rebels in the South and the North when the leaders were arrested.
4 Foreign aid in the form of troops and weapons which were necessary to overthrow the British government did not reach the rebels.
5 Divisions emerged between the United Irishmen. There was tension between Catholic and Presbyterian rural TENANTS, and tension between these tenants and the middle classes.

GET ACTIVE 11

a Consider all the factors explaining the failure of the United Irishmen's rebellion. Complete the grid on the right for all five factors:

Issue to be discussed:			
Factor 1	Level of Importance		
	1 Low	2 Medium	3 High

b Share your findings from your grid with a partner.
c Decide which factor you think was the most important.

WHAT HAPPENED IN IRELAND AFTER THE 1798 REBELLION?

The 1798 rebellion in Ireland frightened the British government, as they realised that their enemy France could use Ireland as a base from which to attack. The British government saw that Ireland needed to be controlled in a tighter way. They planned to close down the Irish parliament by passing the ACT OF UNION in 1801, which meant that Ireland would be ruled only by the parliament in Westminster. At this time Catholics in Britain did not have full political and civil rights. This meant that they could not become MPs or vote.

It had been intended that the Act of Union would be followed by CATHOLIC EMANCIPATION to grant them these rights, but this did not happen. Instead, the Act of Union allowed Ireland to send 100 Protestant MPs to Westminster but no Catholics. This led to discontent. The campaign for the right for Catholics to vote was known as Catholic Emancipation, and it became an important issue in the 1800s. It was not until 1829 that it was granted, when a man called Daniel O'Connell led a campaign for Catholic emancipation through parliament.

Plan, Do, Review

THE REVOLUTION BUG – HOW AND WHY DID IT SPREAD?

In this chapter you have been finding out why revolutions take place, the methods people use to change things, and the effects of revolutions on countries. You have looked at the examples of America and France, where revolutions took place, and then in Ireland where the attempted revolution was not successful.

You are going to design your own visual representation of factors that cause revolutions, how they take place and their consequences.

PLAN

Stage 1

Read carefully over all the work you have done in this chapter. You may find the grid below helps you collect the information you need:

Place	Reasons for (Causes)	Methods	Effects (Consequences) +	-
America				
France				
Ireland				

Remember that one of the consequences of the revolutions in America and France was an attempted revolution in Ireland.

Stage 2

You now have to decide how to represent your information. You could represent your information on three consequence wheels like the one on the left. Your class could be divided into different groups and each group looks at one of the revolutions.

Here are some success CRITERIA, to help you check that you have included the most important things:

- State more than two reasons why the revolution or rebellion broke out.
- Provide at least two examples of how people tried to change things (their methods).
- Show more than two effects of the revolution (its consequences).

DO

Having collected all your evidence and thought about your success criteria, now produce your visual representation. Think carefully about causes, methods and consequences.

Be prepared to present your visual representation and talk about what it means. If you have been working in groups, then each of you will need to plan your individual roles.

REVIEW

Where was your work green? Why did this aspect work well?

In what ways was your work amber? How could you move this aspect to green?

Which aspects of your work were red? How might you try to improve in these aspects?

6 The Great Famine – was it managed appropriately?

In this chapter we are learning to:
- ✓ analyse sources to find out about the past;
- ✓ investigate how history has been used to create stereotypical views;
- ✓ work with others to explore different perspectives.

HOW DO WE DEAL WITH NATURAL DISASTERS TODAY?

Did you know that an earthquake hits the British Isles every four days, on average? That 5 million people in Britain live in areas prone to flooding, and that 10 per cent of the world's population live under threat from over 1,500 active volcanoes? These are all natural hazards. Mostly, they do not cause problems. However, when the natural hazard becomes a real event and impacts on a lot of people, it becomes a 'natural disaster'. Natural disasters are not new. The pictures here show some of the natural disasters that have happened in the past 100 years. What is going on in each of the photographs?

In 2005, Hurricane Katrina hits Louisiana and Mississippi. At least 1,836 people died.

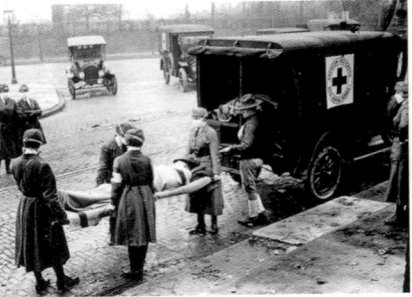

In 1918, a worldwide flu epidemic killed 50–100 million people in just 18 months.

In 2005, over 300,000 people died as a result of a tsunami.

In 1983–5, a famine in Ethiopia led to starvation for 8 million people and 1 million deaths.

1993: Storm of the Century – A blizzard on the east coast of the USA resulted in 300 deaths and $6.6 billion of damage.

In 2001, Foot and Mouth epidemic – 7 million sheep and cattle were killed. The crisis cost Britain £8 billion.

GET ACTIVE 1

a Your task is to find out more about one of the disasters shown in the photos on the left by copying and completing the table below. You could ask some older members of your family if they remember some of the more recent events, or you could try searching the internet – perhaps a site like Wikipedia would be a good starting point.

Date	Disaster	What happened?	Who was affected?	Reasons for the disaster?	Cost: Lives /Money/ Environmental damage	What did governments do?

b Your teacher will organise a whole-class feedback session. Each time someone else presents, think about (and make notes on): How did governments react to that particular disaster? Did they do enough? Was there anything else they could have done?

c Now in groups, share your ideas. In a group situation, assigning roles (chairperson, scribe, etc.) to each member means that everyone can participate. Once you have agreed what everyone is doing, the group should discuss the following questions:

- Where do you think governments acted appropriately?
- Where do you think they did not act appropriately?
- Should any of these disasters be remembered? Why?
- What can we achieve by remembering the past?
- Are there any downsides to remembering the past?

How can a natural disaster be managed?

If a major natural disaster such as a famine happens today, different people think and respond differently, as suggested in the thought bubbles.

Famine hits Africa yet again

Organise a concert to raise money

Censor the media so people don't find out about it.

Do nothing.

Have emergency plans and put them into operation.

I need to do something, otherwise I'll lose support, but should I increase taxes?

Create some real and permanent jobs.

GET ACTIVE 2

a Can you think of any additional responses to the ones suggested?

b What factors shape our different responses to natural disasters?

c Governments are sometimes criticised for their handling of such crises. Why are governments often slow to manage such crises?

HOW DID WE DEAL WITH NATURAL DISASTERS IN THE PAST?

The Case of the Great Irish Famine

From 1845 to 1849 Ireland experienced a GREAT FAMINE, when a disease called *phythophtera infestans* – more commonly called the 'blight' – struck the potato crop. The disease was widespread across Europe, and caused hardship and deaths in many countries such as Germany and the Netherlands, but in Ireland it resulted in disaster.

Around one-third of the Irish population, mainly in the west of Ireland, relied almost completely on potatoes for survival. Before the disease struck, this was not a problem. In fact, cultivation of potatoes permitted a reasonable standard of living by contemporary standards. The nutritional content of the potato, and easy access to turf for heating fuel, meant that people in Ireland were healthier and lived longer than the poor in other parts of Europe at the time. However, because the Irish were so dependent on the potato, it meant that when the crop failed there was no alternative food available. Shorter famines had struck Ireland before, but the one that occurred in 1845 was longer lasting and more widespread.

GET ACTIVE 3

Look at the census statistics on the illustration.

a Can you calculate exactly how many people died, according to the census figures?

b Do you think these are accurate figures? Why do you think so?

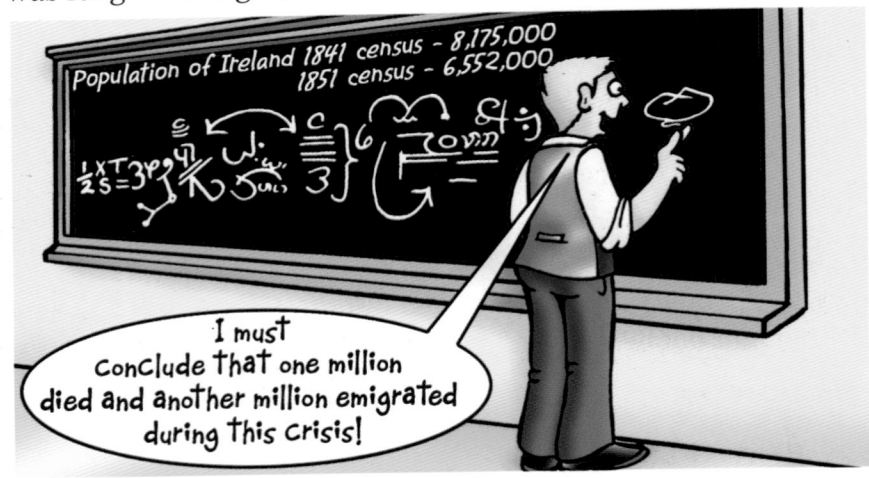

How was this disaster managed?

Just as with the government response to many modern disasters, the government's response to the Irish famine has been severely criticised, both at the time and since. For most of the famine crisis, the political party in government were the WHIGS. One of their main ideas was *laissez-faire*; this meant that the government should not interfere with market conditions. To protect the interests of traders and retailers and encourage people to be more self-reliant, the Whigs believed that food should not be provided for free or below market price. The concept of *laissez-faire* was to shape their outlook and actions throughout the famine.

GET ACTIVE 4

A number of different relief measures were introduced to deal with the Irish famine by both the government and private individuals. Working in pairs, consider each of the relief measures that follow on pages 69, 70 and 71. What were the advantages and disadvantages of each? After exploring all the factors, decide which you think was the most effective relief measure. You could use a decision-making grid like the one below to organise your ideas.

Measure	Facts	Positive points	Negative points	What we think about it
Importing corn	Organised by Robert Peel, stopped in 1846 by Lord John Russell	Was successful – no one died from starvation	Irish were not used to cooking/eating corn. Had to come from America – might take a long time to get to Ireland	Good idea, at least no one died, but could they have imported other foods from somewhere closer to Ireland? This might have been cheaper and quicker

Importing corn

At the start of the famine, the Prime Minister, Sir Robert Peel, privately arranged for a £100,000 supply of corn to be sent from America. This was sold to people whose potato crop had failed. The Irish were not familiar with corn and found it difficult to cook and digest. Despite this, the measure was successful and in 1845 and early 1846, no one died from starvation. However, Peel was replaced as prime minister by Lord John Russell in June 1846, and the new government stopped the policy of IMPORTING corn. They were applying the concept of *laissez-faire*. They believed that importing corn might cause a fall in prices at home, and this would not be good for the Irish merchants, on whom they relied for support.

Sir Robert Peel.

Landlords

Lord Roden, a landlord well known for his religious beliefs and his involvement in the ORANGE ORDER, opened a charitable soup shop on his estate selling soup made of rice and meal porridge for a penny a quart, and potato cake at 12 oz. for a penny.

Lord Londonderry, one of the ten richest men in the United Kingdom, owned land in counties Down, Derry, Donegal and Antrim, but gave only £30 to the local relief committee, while spending £150,000 on renovating his house.

Lord Roden.

Lord Londonderry.

The workhouse

Scene at workhouse gate.

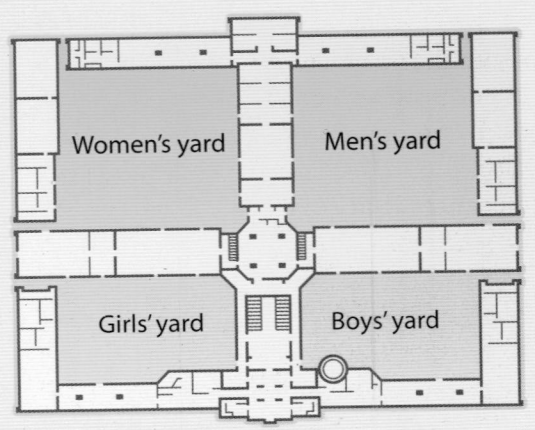

Floor plan of workhouse.

Women's yard

Men's yard

Girls' yard

Boys' yard

This was the main method of relief for most of the famine period, and was established well before the famine. In 1838 the Poor Law Act set up a workhouse system. Ireland was divided into Poor Law Unions, each of which built a workhouse to accommodate people who had nowhere else to go. The workhouses were made as uncomfortable as possible so that people would not want to stay in them. The government believed this would encourage people to rely on themselves rather than the state. Men, women and children lived in separate areas within the workhouse, so families who entered the workhouse were split up. People had to earn their keep by breaking stones, spinning wool or knitting. Two meals a day were provided – a breakfast of oatmeal and buttermilk and a dinner of potatoes and buttermilk.

Public Works

Office of Public Works in Dublin as it is today.

The Prime Minister, Lord John Russell, and his Whig colleagues believed in the virtues of hard work, thrift and self-reliance. In August 1846 they announced that the Irish poor would not receive handouts, but would have to work for wages which they could then use to buy food. Under the Public Works scheme, the government employed the starving to work on projects such as building roads, canals and walls, but the pay was insufficient to feed a family. Sometimes the projects were not constructive – for example, filling in valleys and flattening hills. By 1847, over 700,000 men were employed in public works schemes. The hours were long, and because the labourers had little food they did not have the energy needed for the work. The costs of the schemes were to be covered by the local rates. There were difficulties in administering the payments, so at times workers were paid late or not paid at all. The attraction of paid work also encouraged the poor to move away from their homes, so they did not continue farming at home. This increased the food shortage.

Soup kitchens

Making soup in a Quaker kitchen.

In the spring of 1847, the government set up soup kitchens, which were to feed the starving until the next harvest. Due to administration difficulties, the soup kitchens were established slowly, but by August 1847 over 3 million people a day were being fed. The 'soup' was a type of watery porridge. The soup kitchens marked a major change in the government's approach to relief. However, only people who had under a quarter of an acre of land were eligible. Those without any income were given the soup free of charge. Those who were earning wages had to purchase it. The scheme was suspended in September 1847 when the famine appeared to be over.

The QUAKERS set up soup kitchens and also gave grants for relief, distributed through both Protestant and Catholic clergymen. From 1848, the Quakers became involved in providing longer-term assistance, such as fishing tackle, seeds and farm implements. The Quakers were personally involved in distributing famine relief, and this often had personal consequences. At least fifteen Quakers died as a result of famine-related diseases and many more, including Joseph Bewley (the coffee merchant), died prematurely as a result of exhaustion.

Women

Mary-Ann McCracken.

Women were very active in providing relief during the famine. This was at a time when women did not have equality with men. Women's groups were set up in Ireland and England. One of the most successful was the Belfast Ladies' Association, a group of women of all religious DENOMINATIONS. A prominent member of the women's group was Mary-Ann McCracken. She led a long and active life dedicated to various causes, such as the welfare of women and children, and the abolition of slavery, until her death in 1866 at the age of 96. Her brother, Henry Joy, had been executed for his part in the 1798 rebellion. Mary-Ann and the Belfast Ladies' Association's achievements were:

- creating committees to collect money and distribute relief;
- setting up food kitchens;
- establishing an Industrial School to teach girls skills such as spinning, knitting and needlework, which would help them find jobs.

GET ACTIVE 5

Your task is to find out and write a short paragraph about Mary-Ann's life and achievements. Before you begin your research, think about the questions you want to find out about (e.g. Was she also involved in the 1798 rebellion? What was her relationship with her brother really like? What were the key events in Mary-Ann's personal life? What did she accomplish? etc.) Good places to start finding answers are the internet, your school or local library, or local historical association.

WHAT DID PEOPLE *AT THE TIME* THINK OF THE GOVERNMENT'S RESPONSE TO THE FAMINE?

The government's management of the famine in Ireland has been the subject of CONTROVERSY both at the time and since. Some people claimed that the government did not care about Ireland and willingly allowed people to die, others have criticised more strongly, claiming that a policy of GENOCIDE was deliberately pursued. Others have argued that the government's response was ineffective but must be seen in the context of the time, with prevalent ideas such as *laissez-faire*, and the difficulties of both gathering accurate information and administering relief when communications were not good.

Sources 1–4 reflect the views of some people who witnessed the famine.

SOURCE 1

The Almighty indeed sent the potato blight but the English created the famine ... A million and half men, women and children were carefully, prudently and peacefully slain by the English government. They died of hunger in the midst of abundance which their own hands created.

John Mitchel, The Last Conquest of Ireland (Perhaps) (1861)

SOURCE 2

This illustration was drawn by James Mahony, who was employed by the *London Illustrated News* to provide images of conditions in Ireland.

SOURCE 3

We are aware that our excellent and humane Lord Lieutenant is making every effort to aid the people.

The Waterford Freeman, 3 October 1846

SOURCE 4

I am well aware of the deep anxiety you felt for our destitute people, and your efforts to save them from the effects of the destruction of the potato crop last season. Famine would have destroyed this country were it not for your wise actions.

From a letter written by Father Theobald Mathew (Cork) to Charles Trevelyan, 7 August 1846

GET ACTIVE 6

a Which sources support the notion that the government did not do enough?
b Which suggests that the government acted appropriately to help relieve famine?
c Which views do you agree with? Why? What evidence do you have to support your view?
d Study Source 4. What questions would you like to ask Father Mathew? You might use these starters to help you: Who? What? Where? Why? When? How?
e Using the sources and your own ideas, do you think people at the time thought the government managed the famine appropriately?

WHAT DO PEOPLE *TODAY* THINK OF THE GOVERNMENT'S RESPONSE TO THE FAMINE?

SOURCE 5

The government used the famine as an opportunity to facilitate various long-desired changes within Ireland. These included population control and the consolidation of property through various means, including emigration.

Historian Christine Kinealy in her book
This Great Calamity, 1997

SOURCE 6

Famine mural in west Belfast.

SOURCE 7

By a lonely prison wall,

I heard a young girl calling,

"Michael, they have taken you away

For you stole Trevelyan's corn

So the young might see the morn'

Now a prison ship lies waiting in the bay."

Lyrics from a folk song 'The Fields of Athenry',
written by Pete St John in the 1970s. The song tells
the story of Michael, who was sent to Australia for
stealing food to feed his starving family.

SOURCE 8

Those who governed in London at the time failed their people through standing by while a crop failure turned into a massive human tragedy. That 1 million people should have died in what was then part of the richest and most powerful nation in the world is something that still causes pain as we reflect on it today.

Tony Blair (Prime Minister), June 1997

GET ACTIVE 7

Your task is to explore Sources 5–8 to find out about how the famine is remembered today.

a Start by using the '5W' method (asking Who? What? Why? When? and Where?) which you have used before to explore historical evidence.

b Now, you're ready to dig a bit deeper. Let's think a bit more about the attitudes behind these sources. Look again at each of the sources in turn. Think about why each person created it. What might have been the intention? What might they hope to have achieved by doing this? What do they state explicitly in their source? What is suggested or inferred?

c Often, events in the past can be selectively presented. This means that not all the information about an event is given, in the hope that other people can be persuaded to believe a particular point of view. Look again at the sources here. Do you think any of them have tried to portray the famine in a deliberately selective way? If so, why do you think they have done this?

Plan, Do, Review

This chapter has focused on how natural disasters, present and past, have been managed. You will now appreciate that different people have different points of view on how the Irish famine was managed by the government of the time.

Your task is to create a radio or TV talk show about the famine and the relief that was provided at the time. Your show will explore a range of different perspectives. These can be the views of people who lived at the time, or the views of people living today.

PLAN

Stage 1

As a class, decide whether you want to explore the views of people at the time, or people today. Your teacher will divide the class into groups, with each group representing a different perspective on the famine. Look back over this chapter and note the range of views. If you are exploring contemporary views, you could have:

- a family who were starving
- a contemporary woman, such as Mary-Ann McCracken
- a member of the British government.

And so on ...

If you are exploring the views of people today, you might have:

- a historian, such as Christine Kinealy
- Tony Blair
- the creator of the famine mural.

And so on ...

You will also need one group to play the role of the talk show host.

Stage 2

You need to become familiar with how talk shows work. Listen to or watch some at home to get an idea of what goes on. Think about what makes a good show (e.g. people being asked to explain or defend their views, rather than just expressing them). Jot down some points to help you remember!

Stage 3

Your group task will be to summarise the views of your particular character. Think about the questions you need to ask yourselves:

- What was his/her name?
- What would he/she have thought of the relief measures?
- Would he/she have expected the government to do more?
- Why?

And so on. You need to have a really good understanding of your character and his/her thoughts and feelings.

DO

Your teacher will organise the talk show and perhaps record it to help you with your review!

REVIEW

Take some time to reflect on this activity. Write a short report on it, considering three areas:

1 Your learning about this period of history. What have you learned in terms of historical knowledge, skills and understanding?
2 Your contribution to the group's work. What did you do? How did you do it? What did you do well? Are there any areas for improvement? If you had to do the same activity again, would you do anything differently?
3 Working as a group. How did your group do? Could you have done better? What would help you do better as a group next time?

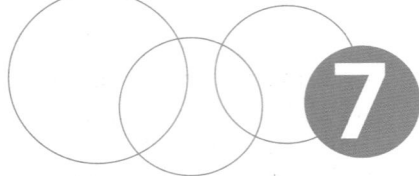

7 Who made a difference and how?

In this chapter we are learning to:
- ✓ make connections across different periods of history;
- ✓ explore different points of view;
- ✓ think creatively and develop your problem-solving skills.

You will already be familiar with the ACT OF UNION which joined Ireland with Great Britain (see page 63). In the years that followed, a number of people attempted to reverse this Act. They wanted to make a difference to how Ireland was governed. Some wanted Ireland to have her own PARLIAMENT but to remain within the United Kingdom; others wanted a complete break with Britain. Those who wanted to overturn the Act of Union used different approaches and methods to try to get what they wanted. This chapter looks at three attempts.

DANIEL O'CONNELL

Name: Daniel O'Connell, a.k.a. 'The Liberator'

Born: 1775

Died: 1847

Aims:
- CATHOLIC EMANCIPATION – At this time, Catholics could not be elected to the parliament at Westminster.
- Repeal of the Act of Union – Overturning this Act would give Ireland control over her own internal government (but not foreign affairs).

Methods: Hated violence – was committed to peaceful methods. Held huge rallies called 'monster meetings' as a peaceful means of expressing views and pressurising the government. The largest one took place in Tara, Co. Meath in 1843 when half a million people gathered.

Achievements/legacy: 1829 Catholic Emancipation Act – granted full civil and political rights to Roman Catholics.

Failed to achieve Repeal of the Act of Union. Cancelled a monster meeting at Clontarf, Dublin in response to a government ban on the meetings. After this, his influence weakened.

Daniel O'Connell was born in County Kerry in 1775. He was educated partly in France, and while he was there the French Revolution took place (see pages 56–9). This had a huge impact on O'Connell. The bloodshed convinced him that peaceful rather than violent means were the only way to achieve anything. O'Connell returned to Ireland and had a very successful career as a barrister. He was in Ireland when the United Irishmen staged their rebellion, but he did not support it. After the Act of Union was passed in 1801, Ireland elected representatives to the parliament at Westminster, but Catholics were excluded. They were not allowed to sit in the parliament. In the 1820s, O'Connell began to work for Catholic Emancipation with the support of the Catholic Church. In 1828 O'Connell was elected as the MP for Clare, and in 1829 Catholic Emancipation was granted.

After this success O'Connell turned his attention to the Act of Union, and began a campaign to have it repealed. O'Connell did not want a complete break with Britain. He wanted an independent Kingdom of Ireland with a parliament in Dublin that would govern itself, and which would recognise Queen Victoria as the Queen of Ireland. O'Connell organised huge rallies called 'monster meetings' as a peaceful means of expressing views. However, the government became alarmed about the possibility of public riots and banned a meeting which was to be held in Clontarf, Dublin on 8 October 1843. Rather than risk potential violence and bloodshed, O'Connell called off the meeting, and this marked the beginning of the end of the Repeal movement. O'Connell was arrested and spent three months in prison. In 1845 the Repeal movement split between those who supported O'Connell and peaceful methods, and a group of younger men who wanted to use violence to end the union. O'Connell's time in prison affected his health and he died in 1847 while on his way to Rome.

GET ACTIVE 1

Sources 1–3 reflect the views of three historians on O'Connell and his achievements.

a Study Source 1. According to Rees, who benefited from O'Connell's achievements? Do you think this historian would agree that O'Connell deserves the title of 'The Liberator'?

b Study Source 2. What does Beckett say about O'Connell's methods? Refer back to Chapter 5. Why do you think France and the US were sympathetic to the cause of Repeal?

c According to all the sources, what were O'Connell's main achievements?

d What difference do you think O'Connell made? (Think about the impact he made, both short- and long-term.)

SOURCE 1

The Emancipation Act opened up nearly every public office to Catholics. The main beneficiaries were members of the Catholic MIDDLE CLASS. For the peasantry, the foot soldiers of the agitation, there was no material gain.

Russell Rees

SOURCE 2

O'Connell's monster meetings demonstrated his splendid oratory, the popularity of the movement and his power to control it. Though hundreds of thousands gathered to hear him, and though he used the most inflammatory language, there was never … any sign of disorder. All this was very damaging to the prestige of the government, not only at home but abroad; in France and in the United States there was a good deal of sympathy for the repeal cause, and O'Connell became a figure of international importance.

J.C. Beckett

SOURCE 3

Daniel O'Connell's Repeal Party and the Young Irelanders laid the grounds for a nationalist movement.

Brian Walker

YOUNG IRELAND MOVEMENT

Thomas Davis   **John Mitchel**   **William Smith O'Brien**

Name: Young Ireland movement, a.k.a. the Irish Confederation. Prominent members were Thomas Davis, Charles Gavan Duffy, Thomas Francis Meagher, John Mitchel and William Smith O'Brien.

Influences: Were inspired by the 1848 revolutions in France, Italy and Germany and the 1798 rebellion in Ireland.

Aim: Complete INDEPENDENCE for Ireland.

Methods: Thought that a violent revolution was the only way to achieve their aims.

Achievements/legacy: Their attempt at a rebellion in 1848 failed, but the ideas and methods of the Young Ireland movement inspired later generations of Irish Republicans.

The Young Ireland movement emerged from O'Connell's Repeal movement. It consisted of a small group of INTELLECTUALS who became disillusioned with O'Connell's peaceful methods, and argued that only a violent revolution could end the Union. Unlike O'Connell, the Young Ireland movement wanted complete independence for Ireland. Its members were both Protestant and Catholic. They were strongly influenced by events in France, and in 1848 two of the leaders – Meagher and O'Brien – went to France to study revolutionary events there. They returned with a new flag for Ireland. The design – a tricolour of orange, white and green – was similar to the present Irish flag, with the addition of the red hand of Ulster in the white area.

The most militant member of the group was John Mitchel, an Ulster Protestant. In 1847 Mitchel established a journal called the *United Irishman* to help spread radical ideas and build support for an armed uprising. The success of the French Revolution of February 1848 gave the Young Ireland movement confidence that their approach could be successful. However, the Young Ireland rebellion in 1848 failed miserably. They did not have sufficient arms or widespread support, and Ireland was suffering from famine at this time. Mitchel, Smith O'Brien and Meagher were all transported to Australia.

SOURCE 4

Young Ireland in Business for Himself (*Punch* cartoon).

SOURCE 5

Independence can best be won by a union of all classes, for nationality is broad, comprehensive and universal.

Charles Gavan Duffy, 1847

SOURCE 6

The white in the centre signifies a lasting truce between the 'Orange' and the 'Green', and I trust that beneath its folds the hands of the Irish Protestant and the Irish Catholic may be clasped in generous and heroic brotherhood.

Thomas Francis Meagher, on presenting the flag to the people of Dublin, April 1848

GET ACTIVE 2

a The Young Ireland journal was called the *United Irishman*. Skim back through Chapter 5. What were the similarities and differences between the United Irishmen and the Young Ireland movement?

b Study Source 4. It was published in *Punch*, a British humorous and satirical magazine. What does this cartoon suggest about the Young Irelanders?

c What do Sources 5 and 6 reveal about the Young Irelanders' definition of Irish nationalism?

d What difference do you think the Young Ireland movement made? (Again, think about both short- and long-term impact.)

e The flag which Meagher and O'Brien brought back from France was intended to represent all the people of Ireland, and gave Ulster prominence (the red hand of Ulster was placed in the centre). Which symbols would you include in a new flag for Northern Ireland? Why would you include them? Design a new flag, or a government letterhead, that represents the people of Northern Ireland.

CHARLES STEWART PARNELL

No man has the right to set bounds to the march of a nation. No man can say to his country – thus far shalt thou go and no further.

Part of a speech given by Parnell in Cork, January 1885

Name: Charles Stewart Parnell, a.k.a. 'The Uncrowned King of Ireland'

Born: 1846

Died: 1891

Aims: Wanted 'Home Rule' – a parliament for Ireland with control over internal affairs.

Methods: Obstruction. To force MPs to focus on Ireland, Parnell used this tactic in parliament. It consisted of holding up parliamentary business by talking for hours at a time, sometimes all through the night.

Achievements/legacy: Leader of the Irish Parliamentary Party 1879–90.
President of the Land League.
Strengthened the Irish Parliamentary Party and turned it into the first 'modern' political party.
Gave Ireland more prominence in British politics.

THE IRISH FRANKENSTEIN.

The Irish Frankenstein (*Punch* cartoon).

GET ACTIVE 3

a Parnell stated that he wanted Home Rule, not a completely independent Ireland. Study Source 7: does this speech support his claim?

b Study Source 8. Explain what the cartoonist is suggesting about Parnell. Does Source 8 agree with Source 7?

c What difference did Parnell make? (Again, think about both short- and long-term impact.)

Charles Stewart Parnell came from an ANGLO-IRISH land-owning family. In 1879, he took over the Home Rule Party and immediately restructured it. Parnell changed its name to the IRISH PARLIAMENTARY PARTY, imposed a strict party oath obliging its MPs to vote as a group, and gained financial support from the Irish in America. The party can be seen as the first modern political party in Britain, and the main British parties eventually modelled their own party structures on Parnell's example. Parnell also played a significant role in the LAND LEAGUE established by Michael Davitt in 1879 with the goal of land reform. Parnell became the first president of the organisation, and this ensured the support of small farmers.

A HOME RULE BILL was introduced into parliament in 1886. It had the support of the Liberal Prime Minister, Gladstone. However, the Bill failed. Despite its failure, the Home Rule Bill was a success for Parnell, as it gave the issue of Irish Home Rule prominence in British politics.

Parnell's personal life was to lead to his downfall. In 1880 Parnell had become involved in a love affair with Katherine (Kitty) O'Shea, the wife of another Home Rule MP, Captain William O'Shea. The subsequent divorce led to a split within the party. The Catholic Church was very critical of Parnell, and Gladstone refused to work with him. Shortly after this, Parnell became seriously ill and died in 1891 at the age of 45.

UNIONIST REACTION

We have looked at three examples of people who wanted to overturn the Act of Union. Action was also taken by those who wanted to maintain the Union. In the 1870s, as the Home Rule movement became stronger, unionist resistance to this became more evident. One man who tried to make a difference by working to maintain the Union was Colonel Edward Saunderson, a Cavan landlord and the MP for North Armagh.

Colonel Saunderson became convinced that unionists must organise themselves to resist Home Rule and use arms if necessary. When, at the end of 1885, Gladstone, the British Prime Minister, announced that he would support Home Rule, it seemed that Home Rule for Ireland was inevitable. This spurred Unionist MPs in Parliament to come together to create a separate Irish Unionist party, which was formed in January 1886. Saunderson became the leader of the Irish Unionist Party in the House of Commons and remained at the head of the party until his death in 1906.

At the end of the nineteenth century, Unionism was concerned with the whole of Ireland, not just Ulster. During a debate in the House of Commons on the Home Rule Bill of 1886, it was suggested that in the event of Home Rule being implemented, special terms could be made for Ulster. Saunderson rejected any notion of dividing Ireland.

The Home Rule Bills of 1886 and 1893 produced outbreaks of sectarian rioting. However, this alarmed Saunderson, who wanted a disciplined, controlled response to the issue. A Convention was held in June 1892, and in 1893 the Ulster Defence Union was formed to organise unionists across the country and collect funds. While much of the anti-Home Rule activity was happening in Belfast, it was unionist landlords who led the unionist movement. The distinct character and force of Ulster unionism was only starting to emerge. You will look more closely at Ulster Unionism next year.

The main reasons unionists feared Home Rule were:

- The prosperity of Ulster depended on links with Britain. Raw materials such as coal and iron came from Britain, and the ships and linen produced were sold mainly in Britain or the British EMPIRE.
- Home Rule might mean Rome Rule – would the Catholic Church have a say in government?
- Home Rule might be the first step towards full independence for Ireland and a complete break from Britain.

Name: Edward James Saunderson

Born: 1837

Died: 1906

Aim: To resist 'Home Rule'

Methods: Organised disciplined resistance to Home Rule, but approved of violence if this was deemed necessary

Achievements/legacy: Leader of the Irish Unionist Party

EDWARD SAUNDERSON

SOURCE 9

'On the part of Ulster, and every loyal man in that province, I repudiate that suggestion. We are prepared to stand and fall, for weal or woe, with every loyal man who lives in Ireland.'

Saunderson, 1886, commenting on the possibility of dividing Ireland and excluding Ulster from Home Rule

GET ACTIVE 4

Study the main reasons why unionists feared Home Rule.

a Which do you think is the most important? Why?

b Can you think of other reasons why people might object to Home Rule?

c Study Source 9. What does it tell you about Saunderson's attitude to:
   - Ulster?
   - The use of violence?

d What difference did Sanderson make? (Again, think about both the short- and long-term impact.)

Plan, Do, Review

This chapter has focused on how some people wanted to make a difference. Your task is to write an obituary for one of the people you encountered in this chapter. An obituary is a notice of a person's death. It is usually published in a newspaper, and includes a short biography, detailing achievements and the type of person they were. Obituaries generally include both factual information and opinion.

PLAN

Stage 1

Decide who you want to write about. Skim through the chapter again. Which of the personalities did you find most interesting? Which do you have a strong opinion about? Which would you like to find out more about?

Stage 2

Once you have decided on the personality you want to write about, conduct some research to find out more about them, then summarise:

- factual details about their life;
- their main achievements;
- your opinion of them.

DO

Choose a partner and agree on what you think makes a good account. It might include some of the following:

- good introduction;
- well organised;
- appropriate information;
- good use of language;
- good expression of personal opinion.

Now, write the obituary. Remember to keep it interesting and to write it as though the reader knows nothing about this person.

REVIEW

With your partner, take turns reading each others' work. Was there evidence of all the features you agreed on? Were any missing? What would you do differently next time you had to write a piece like this?

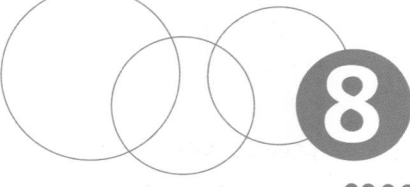

8 Movers and shakers: What enabled people in the past to succeed?

In this chapter we are learning to:
- ✓ understand why people migrate;
- ✓ investigate the characteristics and achievements of entrepreneurs;
- ✓ communicate effectively in a variety of ways.

 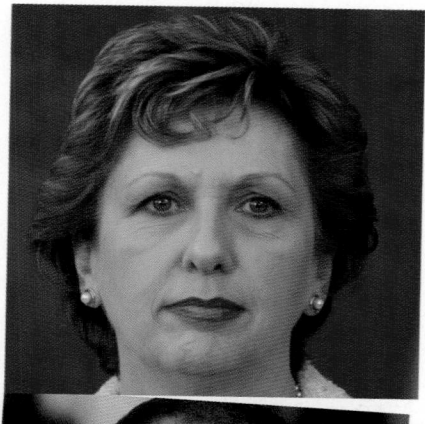

GET ACTIVE 1

a Do you recognise the people in these four photos? Who are they and what do they do?
(If you're really stuck, the answers are in the photo acknowledgements on page 2!)

b What do they have in common?

All the people above are originally from Northern Ireland, but moved away from their local communities in order to be really successful in their chosen fields. Having to move elsewhere, or choosing to do so, is not a new phenomenon. It's been happening in this part of the world for thousands of years! Nearly everyone in your class will have either a relative or know someone else who has moved away from Northern Ireland. People move to another country for many different reasons, but one of the main reasons is to find work. You may also know people who have moved into Northern Ireland in recent years. The experiences of EMIGRANTS and IMMIGRANTS, no matter where they come from or where they go to, are usually very similar.

EMIGRATION

GET ACTIVE 2

In Year 8, you looked at inward migration into Ireland. Can you remember who moved into Ireland? Create a visual representation of the different groups who came to Ireland and when they came. Use the images below to help you get thinking!

GET ACTIVE 3

a Your task is to find out about emigration in your family. To begin an enquiry, you will need to think of the questions you might ask. In pairs, decide on five key things you want to find out about your family's emigration experience, and then develop questions that will draw out the kind of information you need. Try to think of open-ended questions – questions that require the respondent to give information rather than yes/no answers. For example, if 'destination' is one of your key areas, you might ask 'Where did they go?' rather than 'Did they go to Australia?'

b Now, as a class, agree on the five key questions that everyone will ask their relatives. When you ask the questions, you might find it easier to record the answers rather than write down all the information.

c Represent your findings in a way that is meaningful to you. You might want to make a spidergram, use symbols, or write a paragraph. The important thing is to record as much information as you can about your family's experience.

d Now, it's time to bring together all the class findings. Your teacher will organise this, and suggest ways that you can record the class experience. You might do this in graph, table or other form.

e Now, draw some conclusions from your class findings. These will depend on the questions you asked, but you should be able to find out popular destinations, reason for going, methods of travel etc.

When people think about Irish emigration, they tend to associate this with the GREAT FAMINE (see Chapter 6) and people being forced to leave their homes or face starvation.

In fact, it would be a mistake to think that most people who left Ulster in the past did so because they had no other options. Emigration from Ulster began in the eighteenth century. One of the earliest documented cases of emigration was that of a group of PRESBYTERIANS who left Lifford, Co. Donegal in 1705 and settled in Philadelphia. From 1815, the number of people leaving Ulster increased. These emigrants left voluntarily – they were the movers and shakers of their time. They went on to have successful lives in Canada and the United States.

GET ACTIVE 4

On pages 85–6, you will find information about emigration from Ulster to Canada (known as British North America at the time) in the period before 1845. Your task is to build up a picture of a typical Ulster emigrant to Canada at this time. You will need to read the question boxes and pick out the main points to help build up your picture.

AMERICA

THE RACHEL

VIA THE ATLANTIC

Will sail from Belfast and weather permitting, on or about

AUGUST 14th

Johnston & Sons Shipping Co.

Who went?

Different types of people went to different destinations. Most of the people who crossed the Atlantic to Canada and the United States were reasonably well off. In 1815, it cost almost £50 to take a family of four across the Atlantic, although by 1845, because of the number of ships crossing the Atlantic, the price had fallen to around £4 per passenger.

In contrast, the journey to Liverpool took less than a day and the fare was a shilling (there were 20 shillings to the pound), so those who were poor generally went to Britain. However, even though these emigrants were poor, they were people who had initiative and courage. Well before the famine, there was already an established pattern of men travelling to Britain to work as seasonal labourers for harvest time, or for railway or canal building projects and after 1820, a regular steamship service across the Irish Sea made Britain a very accessible destination.

Where did they go?

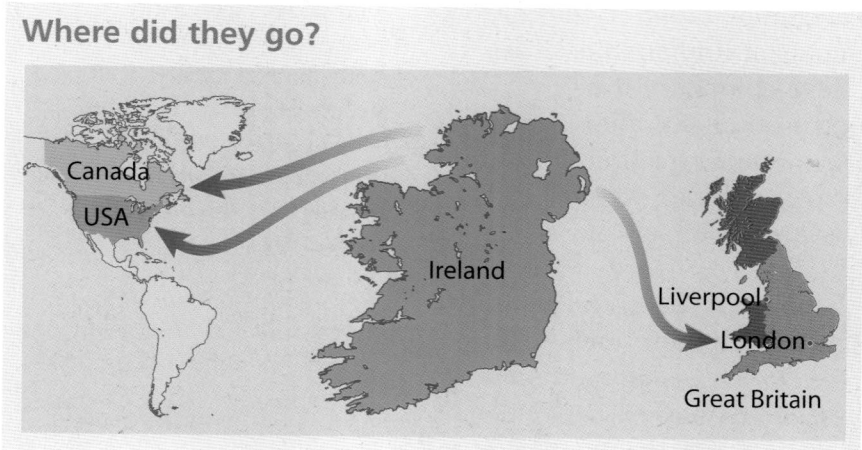

Canada
USA
Ireland
Liverpool
London
Great Britain

How many went?

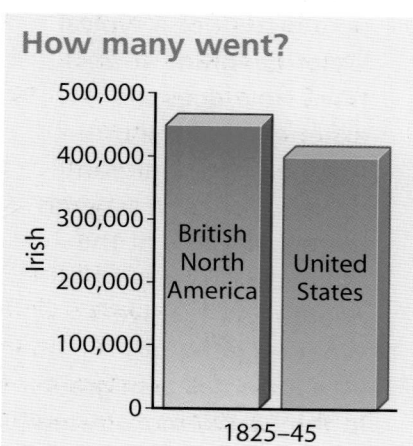

1825–45

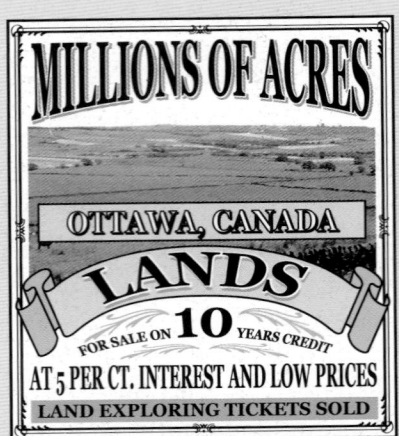

SOURCE 1

Dear Sister,
I understand by your letter that you are willing to come to America if you had the means of coming. I send you in this letter four pounds sterling which is quite adequate to bring you to this country. I hope you will take care of it and lay it out to the best advantage.

Mary Duggan, a maid in Kingston, Upper Canada, writing in 1847 to her sister in Dungiven, Co. Londonderry

Why did they go?

Have you heard of the CELTIC TIGER? It refers to the period of economic growth Ireland has recently experienced. Something very similar happened 200 years ago, at the time of the Napoleonic wars. Ireland's economy boomed, and she exported a lot of grain, linen and other goods to Britain, but this came to an abrupt end in 1815. Once the wars were over, TRADE routes to Europe opened up again and the price of grain fell. This had a very negative impact on Irish farmers. Many switched to different types of farming, such as raising animals. This needed less labour so there were fewer jobs available.

Technological changes in the linen industry also meant that a lot of people who had previously worked in spinning and weaving at home now found that these jobs were no longer available.

While jobs at home became scarcer, jobs in Canada were plentiful, as was land, although land had to be bought. The practice of giving land for free to encourage settlement was virtually over by about 1825.

One of the most important factors in encouraging people to emigrate was the information and support that was provided in letters sent home by friends and relatives who had already emigrated. Such letters provided information about life in the new country, wages and working conditions. Very often the letters contained money which would pay the fares to allow family members to follow. This became known as 'chain migration'.

GET ACTIVE 5

a In Get Active 4, you built up a picture of a typical Ulster emigrant at this time. How does the experience of the pre-famine Ulster emigrant compare or contrast with the experiences of the relatives you found out about in Get Active 3?

b What qualities or attributes have emigrants in the past demonstrated?

How did they go?

All travel at this time was by sea, usually in makeshift accommodation in the cargo holds of timber ships. The development of the transatlantic timber trade was crucial for Irish emigration across the Atlantic. Ships brought timber from North America, and rather than return empty they filled their holds with temporary accommodation for fee-paying passengers.

SOURCE 2

A considerable trade is carried on with the northern states of America. We export partly money, partly linen; we also export the most valuable of all products, the human race. I have heard that this export rated at from four to five thousand annually from the port of Londonderry.

Reverend Vaughan Sampson – Statistical Survey of the County of Londonderry, 1802

WHAT ENABLED PEOPLE IN THE PAST TO SUCCEED?

Retail

Have you heard of Harrods in London? Macy's in New York? Eaton's in Toronto? All are very successful department stores. Eaton's, one of the most important retail businesses in Canada, was started by Timothy Eaton – a man from Ballymena.

Timothy was born in 1834, at Clogher. At the age of thirteen, he was apprenticed to William Smith, a draper and retailer, where he worked fourteen-hour days, slept on a makeshift bed under the counter, and walked the nine miles home on a Sunday. In 1854, as a 20-year-old, Timothy left Ireland to join relatives in southern Ontario, Canada.

Timothy was determined to be successful and in 1860 opened a general store in St Mary's, Ontario. In 1869 he purchased a business in the centre of Toronto, which at the time had a population of 70,000. The new store had a simple policy – selling quality goods at the lowest possible price.

At first the store sold dry goods, but Timothy was keen on taking risks and moved on to sell clothing, household goods and furniture. Timothy was very open to new ideas. He was the first merchant to sell his goods for fixed prices with no haggling, sales for cash only – no credit allowed, and provide a money-back guarantee. In 1883 he opened a much larger store and introduced another new idea – the mail-order catalogue. The catalogues were often the only source of new products for people in rural, isolated areas. They were a huge success and the business expanded rapidly. Eaton's was also the first company to introduce shorter working hours and paid employee holidays.

Timothy died in 1907 aged 72. His son Jack took over the business, which had over 9,000 employees and was worth $5.3 million.

Timothy Eaton.

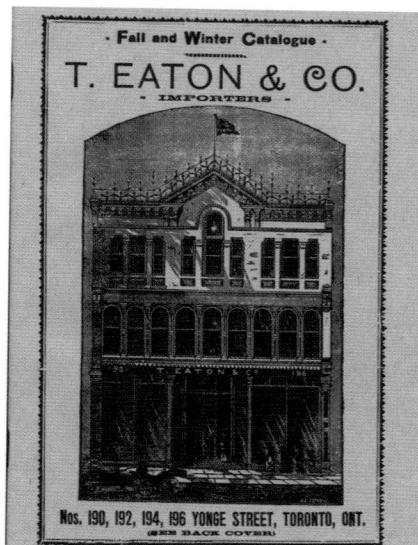
Mail order catalogue.

GET ACTIVE 6

a Below are some of the qualities which the curriculum aims to develop in all young people:

- personal responsibility
- concern for others
- openness to new ideas
- community spirit
- resourcefulness
- moral courage
- determination
- commitment
- self-belief
- pragmatism
- flexibility
- curiosity
- optimism
- respect
- integrity
- tolerance

Which of these attitudes and dispositions do you think Timothy Eaton demonstrated, and how?

b What factors enabled Timothy Eaton to succeed?

Eaton centre, Toronto.

Louis Crommelin.

Linen

Ulster has long had a worldwide reputation for producing high-quality linen goods. The linen industry was already well established, particularly in the Lagan valley, when the HUGUENOTS, who were fleeing RELIGIOUS PERSECUTION in France, arrived in the late seventeenth century. The Huguenots brought skills and expertise and the growth of the linen industry attracted new settlers from England and Scotland. Louis Crommelin introduced new ideas in weaving, and was so successful that King William III appointed him overseer to develop the linen industry.

At this time, linen was mostly produced on a small scale by people in their own homes. The work was carried out mainly by women and children to supplement the family income. In the nineteenth century, the industry was transformed from a cottage-based one to one which was centered in mills and factories. Technological change and the development of mechanised spinning and power-looms for weaving led to the building of many factories. They were mainly situated at the docks in Belfast or close to railway lines and canals which transported the coal needed to power the machines.

By 1900, linen employed 78,000 workers – nearly 70 per cent of these were women. Working conditions were bad. The machinery was powered by steam, and damp conditions often caused lung diseases.

Numbers employed in mills	
1840	8,000
1900	78,000

GET ACTIVE 7

a When people who don't live here hear about Northern Ireland, what do they think of? What sort of reputation does Northern Ireland have today? What is it best known for? Is it a fair reputation?

b Do you wear, use or have anything that was made in Northern Ireland? What sorts of goods and services do we produce here today?

Cottage industry.

Shipbuilding

Have you been to the Titanic quarter in Belfast? If so, you will have seen the site of what was one of the greatest shipbuilding centres in the world.

It began back in the 1850s, when Edward Harland, an English engineer, opened a shipyard in Belfast, and in 1861 the partnership of Harland and Wolff was created. The success of the shipyard was a result of their creative and innovative designs. Harland and Wolff developed the flat-bottomed cargo ship. The other big yard in Belfast, Workman and Clarke, pioneered refrigerated ships. Close links with Britain were a major factor in the success of the shipyards. Harland and Wolff was connected to the White Star line, which was based in Liverpool. The Belfast shipyards had an excellent reputation worldwide, particularly for building luxurious ocean liners. The most famous ship built by Harland and Wolff was the *Titanic*, which sank when it hit an iceberg in 1912.

Numbers employed in shipbuilding	
1860	500
1914	14,000

The *Titanic*.

GET ACTIVE 8

Like Timothy Eaton, the movers and shakers at home had qualities and attributes that enabled them to become successful.

a What qualities do you think people like Crommelin, Harland and Wolff had?

b What other factors contributed to their success?

c Your task is to design a leaflet to promote Ulster's goods at the end of the nineteenth century.

- First, do the research! How does Northern Ireland promote its products today? Investigate the work of agencies tasked to do this. Analyse some modern leaflets. What are the key features?

- Apply what you have learned to the goods Ulster produced at the end of the nineteenth century.

Plan, Do, Review

In this chapter, you have been learning about how people from Ulster made an impact in the past – both at home and abroad. Your task is to write a 250-word report for the government on the contribution of people from Ulster to economic development in the nineteenth century, at home and abroad.

PLAN

Stage 1 – Gather your thoughts

- Skim back through this chapter. Make some notes.
- What did people achieve:
  - at home?
  - abroad?
- What qualities and characteristics did people have?

Stage 2 – Plan your report

- Decide on the most interesting way to present your ideas. Remember you are limited to 250 words. Think about whether you also want to use pictures or symbols.
- How many paragraphs will you have? What will each one focus on?
- What key points/descriptive words do you want to include?

DO

- Write your report.
- Remember to keep within the 250-word limit.
- Remember that this is a report for the government, so make sure your writing is appropriate for the audience.
- Once you have written your initial draft, check it over to see if you can improve it.

REVIEW

- Re-read your report and the comments your teacher has made.
- What did you do well?
- What do you wish you had done better?
- Jot down two ideas that will help you improve your work next time you do something similar.

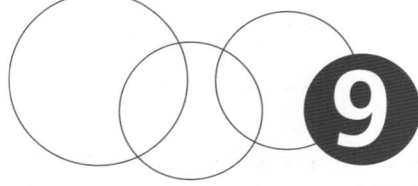

9 Getting better at history

 In this chapter we are learning to:
✓ set our own targets for improvement in history;
✓ use an assessment grid to assess others' work;
✓ contribute to a class discussion.

You began this book by investigating the big changes that occurred in the period and the reasons why some were more significant than others. Which event or person do you think has been the most significant for you?

WHAT HAVE YOU LEARNED FROM YOUR STUDY OF IRELAND 1500–1900?

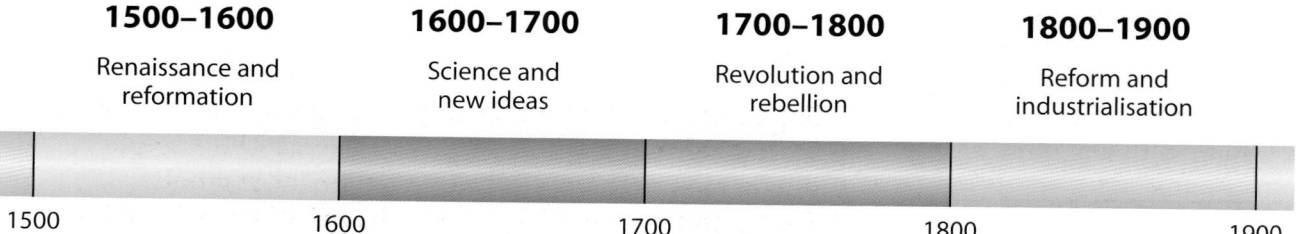

1500–1600	1600–1700	1700–1800	1800–1900
Renaissance and reformation	Science and new ideas	Revolution and rebellion	Reform and industrialisation

1500   1600   1700   1800   1900

GET ACTIVE 1

a Each century is characterised by its key events, changes and developments. For you, which are the most significant and least significant? Give reasons for your choices.

b Now try answering these questions, as a way of summarising the period you have just studied.
  • Who were the important people in the period?
  • Did anybody ever conquer Ireland after the Flight of the Earls in 1607?
  • What changes did the new PLANTATIONS in the sixteenth and seventeenth centuries bring to Ireland?
  • Why did Ireland not have its own revolution?

c And finally, think of endings to these starter phrases.
  • My favourite examples of people who made a difference in the nineteenth century were …
  • Ireland sought help from abroad in this period because …
  • A famous nineteenth-century female figure was …
  • The years 1500–1900 were a time of …

GET ACTIVE 2

a Look at the 20 words on the right for 20 seconds.

b Turn your book over and write down as many words as you can remember.

c Now look at the answers and give yourself a score out of twenty:
0–10 average
10–16 very good
16–20 exceptionally good.

d Think about how you remembered the information. Share your score and your techniques with a partner. What other ways of remembering information have you found out about, e.g. could you do the same thing with key dates?

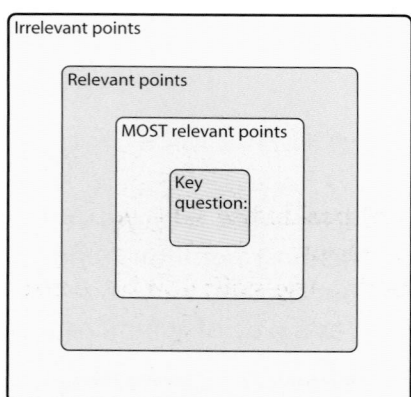

Irrelevant points
Relevant points
MOST relevant points
Key question:

DEVELOPING THE RIGHT SKILLS TO STUDY HISTORY

1 Memory

Being a good student in history requires a good memory to be able to recall all the things that you have learned. How good is your memory, and **how** do you recall the information when you need it? Get Active 2 includes one way in which you could test how good your memory is.

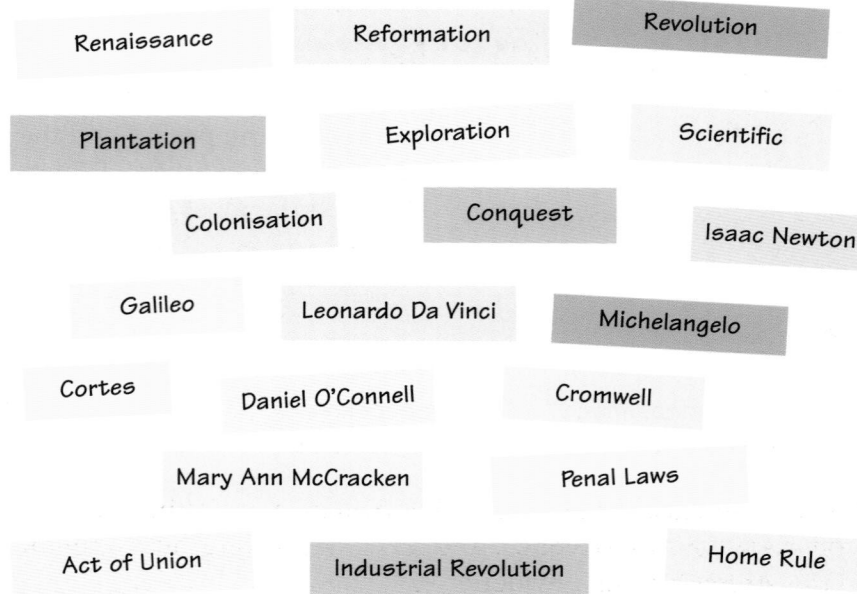

Renaissance   Reformation   Revolution

Plantation   Exploration   Scientific

Colonisation   Conquest   Isaac Newton

Galileo   Leonardo Da Vinci   Michelangelo

Cortes   Daniel O'Connell   Cromwell

Mary Ann McCracken   Penal Laws

Act of Union   Industrial Revolution   Home Rule

2 Selecting, sorting and prioritising

As well as remembering information content, if you are answering a question in an essay or exam you also have to select the most relevant points and reject those that are irrelevant. Prioritising your ideas and information about a key question and justifying your choice is an important skill that you can use in subjects other than history too.

GET ACTIVE 3

a Make a copy of the chart above in your book.

b Read the question below, then work through the seven statements to select which are most relevant or irrelevant to the question. Write their numbers at the most appropriate place on your Zone of Relevance chart.

Why should we study a topic like the plantation of Ulster?

1 It tells us why people on the north coast speak with a Scottish accent.
2 It helps us understand why land is very important to some people in Northern Ireland today.
3 It makes us more tolerant of people who are different to us.
4 It helps us to understand why people in our society today hold very different views about the plantation.
5 It gives us information about the origin of some our town names, like Draperstown.
6 It tells us why some Catholic and Protestant surnames are different.
7 It helps to explain where the word LOYALIST came from.

3 Organising information

Another skill you have to develop in history is how to organise all the information you are given or have researched. Various diagrams have been introduced in the course of this book, e.g. the Venn diagram in Chapter 1 and the mind map in Chapter 3. These grids help you to organise your ideas and thoughts before reaching a conclusion, or to pull your ideas together at the end of a topic.

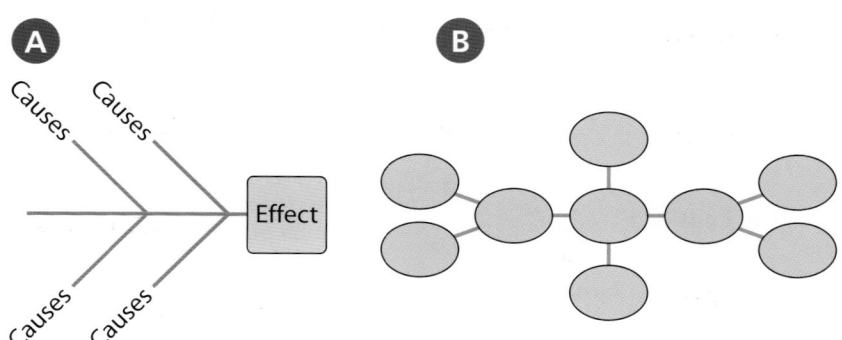

GET ACTIVE 4

Match the number of each of the topics below to the letter of the grid you think would be the most useful.

1 A list of causes which led to the French Revolution.
2 Advantages, disadvantages and interesting points about famine relief in the nineteenth century.
3 The consequences of the Protestant REFORMATION on Ireland.
4 What factors influenced William III's decision to invade Ireland in 1690?

4 Other historical skills of using evidence

Finally, there are the skills of using evidence, weighing the INTERPRETATIONS of evidence, and formulating your own opinion on the strength of that evidence.

GET ACTIVE 5

a Make a copy of the Year 9 History Skills wall in your book.
  • Put a green dot beside the skills you know how to use.

  • Put an amber dot beside the skills you need to practise more.
  • Put a red dot beside the skills you have not yet developed.

Checking evidence before believing what I see and read.	Understanding what an interpretation is.	Comparing and contrasting different types of interpretations.	
	Deciding which points are relevant to a particular argument.	Drawing up criteria to decide the significance of certain events and people.	Prioritising changes from the most to the least important.
	Giving several reasons for an event happening, not just one.	Classifying changes into long and short term and their consequences.	Assessing how relevant an important event from the past still is today.

b If you had to decide on the topics for next year's Year 9 course, which of the ones you studied would you keep, and why?

Why did you reject some topics? Are there any other topics not included in this year's work that you would choose?

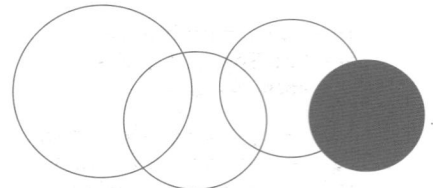

Glossary

Act of Union 1801 The act that made Ireland a part of Britain (the term 'Unionist' is linked to this act)

Anglo-Irish Persons of English descent living in Ireland

Armada A huge fleet of Spanish ships which King Philip of Spain sent to conquer England in 1577

Battle of the Boyne This event took place in 1690, when William of Orange's army defeated that of James II, as part of his Irish campaign

Bawn A wall surrounding a house built during the plantations

Bill A proposed statute which has not yet passed and made law

Catholic Emancipation This was the aim to give Catholics the right to vote

Celtic tiger A name for the period of rapid economic growth in the Republic of Ireland that began in the 1990s

Colony A country or piece of land which is taken and ruled by another state

Commonwealth A form of government with no king – a bit like a republic, and set up in England in the seventeenth century after the execution of King Charles I

Confiscate Take away something

Conspirator A person who takes part in a plot

Constitution A set of principles or rules by which a country is to be governed

Cortes Hernando Cortes was a Spanish explorer who invaded Mexico in 1514 and conquered the civilisation of the Aztecs, taking their great wealth

Criteria The reasons you would use to help you to decide why something is important

Denominations A religious congregation united under a common faith and name

Discursive writing A piece of writing which presents arguments

Emigrant A person who leaves the country of their birth to live permanently in another country

Empire The large amount of territory all over the world that Britain ruled in the nineteenth century. It was the largest in the world

Explorer A person who finds a new place not discovered before

Free Trade This is where trade can take place between countries with no restrictions or duties placed on goods

Genocide The systematic killing of all the people from a national, ethnic or religious group, or an attempt to do this

Great Famine A famine which occurred in Ireland between 1845 and 1849 – also known as the Great Hunger and (in Irish) An Gorta Mór

Home Rule Association Founded in 1873 by Isaac Butt to achieve a parliament for Ireland by peaceful means

Home Rule Bill Bills introduced in 1886, 1893 and 1912 to give Ireland self-government within the UK

Huguenots Name given to the members of the Protestant Reformed Church of France

Immigrant A person living in a country that is not the country of their birth

Import Bring in goods from another country

Independence A country gaining its freedom in order to rule itself

Industrial Revolution The period when steam-powered machines, railways and ships were invented. In the world of work this meant that big machines replaced human labour on the farm and in many industries

Intellectual A person who has a high level of understanding

Interpretation Someone's ideas or version of history

Irish Parliamentary Party Also known as the Home Rule Party. Group of MPs who tried to obtain Home Rule for Ireland

Jacobite The supporters of King James II

Joust A sporting competition between two mounted horsemen with weapons

Land League	Organisation set up by Michael Davitt in 1879. It sought to help tenant farmers own the land they worked on
Loyalist	A person who is loyal to the establishment, who wishes to retain the *status quo*
Martial law	This is when the government places military law on the people
Middle classes	People who tend to work in businesses and professions
Oath of Supremacy	Swearing an oath to recognise the King as the Head of the Church
Orange Order	A Protestant organisation based mainly in Northern Ireland, founded in Loughgall in 1795 and named after the Dutch-born Protestant king of England, William III
Parliament	The body of people who represent others in how a country is ruled
Parliamentarians	A person who supported parliament against King Charles I in the English Civil War
Patriot	A person who is ready to support or fight for their country
Penal Laws	The name given to a set of laws passed in 1691 which deprived both Catholics and Presbyterians of certain rights and liberties, because both groups did not attend the official Church of Ireland services
Pilgrim Fathers	People who went to America in 1620s to set up their own colony and to practise religious freedom
Plantation	The policy of putting settlers in a land in order to control it
Potentate	A ruler with power
Presbyterian	A member of the Presbyterian Church which was set up during the Scottish reformation led by John Knox. Presbyterians believe the church should be governed by a group of elders, not a king
Propaganda	Information, whether true or false, given out in order to influence people to think in a particular way
Protestant Ascendancy	The name for the ruling Anglican class who controlled social, political and economic affairs in Ireland during 1600–1801
Puritans	Those who wanted to purify the Church of England of aspects which they felt were too much like the Roman Catholic Church

Quakers	A Christian denomination founded in England in the seventeenth century
Reformation	Means change, and refers to the change in religion which took place in the sixteenth century where people challenged the authority of the Pope in Rome. In Germany and England this led to the formation of new Protestant religions
Religious persecution	Bad treatment of a group or individual because of their religious beliefs
Renaissance	Means rebirth, and is the name given to the movement which started in Italy around 1500, where scholars began to rediscover ancient knowledge and teachings which had been forgotten for centuries. This led to a development of new ideas in art, sculpture, science and religion
Rent	Payment for the use of something – usually land or property
Revolutionary	A person who is prepared to change things in a country by using force
Significance	The term used to describe why something is important in history
Stormont	The name given to the parliament buildings in Belfast where the first Northern Ireland government was set up in 1921
Tax	This is money which people have to pay for the costs of government
Tenants	People who rent land or property from someone
Tithe	Money paid as a tax to the church
Trade	Buying and selling of goods or services between people or countries
Tyranny	This is unjust, unfair rule of a country benefiting only the wishes of the ruler
Tyrant	A dictator or ruler who is so powerful that people are afraid of them
Undertaker	A settler who came to Ulster and promised to undertake (keep to) the rules of the Ulster plantation
Whigs	Name given to a political grouping, which later became the Liberal party
Woodkerne	Native Irish people

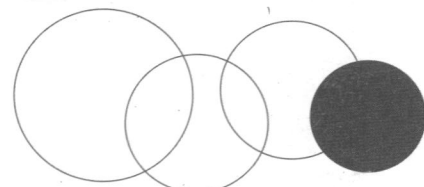

Index